How to

get anything

you want

Just Like That!

Just Like *That* ! How to Get Anything You Want
Author: Janet Poole

Copyright © 2011 Janet Poole

ISBN-13: 978-1439280607

LCCN = 2011911916 (Library of Congress Control Number)

Website: www.janetpoole.com

The author of this book does not dispense medical advice or prescribe the use of any technique as a form of treatment for physical, emotional or medical problems without the advice of a physician, either directly or indirectly. The intent of the author is only to offer information of a general nature to help you in your quest for emotional and spiritual well-being. In the event you use any of the information in this book for yourself, the author and the publisher assume no responsibility for your actions.

Every effort has been made to trace and acknowledge copyright. However, should any infringement have occurred, the publishers tender their apologies and invite copyright owners to contact them.

Disclaimer: Case Studies used in this book are based on real events, but names and details have been changed to protect privacy

Published with the assistance of:
www.loveofbooks.com.au

How to

get anything

you want

Just Like That!

Janet Poole

Mountain View Publishing

Australia

CONTENTS

SECTION 5

Introduction

*D*id you know that you are *entitled* to have *anything* you want? That you *can* have anything you want?

Every human being, including *you*, is precious, remarkable and worthy of having anything they want.

Everything you have in your life comes from *your* thoughts, so another way of looking at it is that right now, you are *getting what* you are *thinking*.

Do you wake up feeling excited about your day? This is how it should be, but many people are confused and discontent about their lives: they feel they are without purpose, they aren't getting what they want and, in most cases, don't feel they are allowed to, or aren't worthy of getting what they want.

In an instant, you can shift to a higher gear, change direction and advance toward a new clarity of purpose, simply by learning practical and easy ways to change your *thoughts*.

'So', you say, 'I will quickly change my thoughts.' And *yes*, that's the whole idea, but it is usually the case that *before* you can change a thought and *hold* the new thought, you need to become aware of the plethora of limiting beliefs, habits and attitudes that lurk behind each thought. If they stay hidden and entrenched, they sabotage your new empowered thought patterns. Change these beliefs and you instantly change your thoughts. This book teaches you what these beliefs are, and it is simply through awareness of them that you naturally start to change your thoughts (and get what you want!).

Does that sound far-fetched? *Not at all!* All you need is an inquiring mind, especially a mind that invites new ideas and considers new ideas promising, exciting and worth trying, and then you *truly can* have *anything you want*.

My Goal: Your Fulfilment

My goal is to motivate you to apply this knowledge in your life. If you do, you will rise each day knowing how marvellous you are, you'll have direction in your life and know it is easy for you to magically create any life you choose. And my job will be done.

A Magnificent Life is Your Choice...

...and if more people chose a magnificent life, Earth would be a happier, more caring and loving place to live. If you are drawn to this information, you are ready to get anything you want. Every person who knows how to take charge of their life and lives it to the best of their ability helps the world in a small yet remarkable way.

"Why Are Some People Happy in Unpleasant Surroundings...

...and others sad in paradise?" This was my favourite question for a long time, and pondering it launched me on my quest to understand life. I persisted with study to expand my understanding of myself, to make sense of how I interacted with the world, discover my reason for being here and fathom the mysterious inner workings of life. I started by assessing why some people's lives are so easy and others so difficult. The conclusions I reached, after many years of work, are exceptionally powerful. They simplify life, they are liberating and, best of all, they are easy to understand.

Challenges Early in My Life...

...were a huge motivator toward greater things. I intuitively knew there was a greater life waiting for me, and I actively searched for new ideas. If they resonated with me, I tried them. As always, life is a great teacher, and I noticed patterns emerging as to how I created my desired outcomes. I felt as if I was turning a ship around with every new way of thinking. My new thoughts and actions kept building on each other, the added strength gradually making my mission easier. Like everyone else in the world I am still constantly changing and evolving towards greater happiness and fulfilment. I have faced extremely tough times in my life and I was horribly confused. But what matters is that I've answered many of my questions and as a result I have achieved a constant state of happiness in my life.

You Are More Empowered...

...to answer your own questions if you understand your role here on Earth, and how life operates. After using this knowledge to help hundreds of people understand their lives, I was motivated to write this book. Too often I meet people who feel lost, without purpose, who battle with their relationships, face unnecessary daily challenges and live in fear. Through this book, you will discover your reason for being here, gain greater clarity on how to breeze through any issues and have fun doing it. You will then be empowered to create your *own* dream life.

The Domino Effect of Your Thoughts

It only takes one or two powerful revitalizing thought patterns to create a domino effect on the rest of your life. Everything in your life is connected.[1] Once you grasp the power of your thoughts, you can create anything you choose.

My Website at Your Service Every Day

For additional information about this book and subject, to ask questions or make comments (I love questions and comments), please visit my website www.janetpoole.com.

Enjoy the book, I wrote it for you,
with love,
Janet

How This Book Works

There Is No Right or Wrong Way…only *Your* Way

This book will liberate you from everything you thought you *had* to do. Now you will discover that you can do what you *want* to do, what you *love* to do. Freedom is a tremendous high, just like a drug, except freedom is healthy…and eternal.

Be gentle with yourself on this path, as there is no right or wrong way to live your life. Each way you choose merely supplies feedback for you, only learning. The life experience that each of us requires is unique. There are many different paths you can take, and you are entitled to those choices.

The biggest blessing you can give someone is to accept them for who they are. Start by accepting *yourself*, and go with what resonates for *you*.

Release Those Unwanted Attitudes

To get what you want, first you need to become aware of what you are *currently* thinking. This book introduces easy-to-understand elements of quantum physics, which unlock new concepts enabling you to release those unwanted attitudes and blaze a trail to the life you want. You are also provided with new skills to empower your life, and you are given recipes to produce what you want.

This Book Simplifies Life

This book uses simple methods that can be replicated in all areas of your life. Your questions are answered clearly, and the mystery of life disappears in a flash. By choosing to use this knowledge, you increase your wisdom and you stamp out fear and drama from your life. You'll have direction and the tools to create your dream life and get whatever you want. However, it's essential to know that you are in charge of your life, and to believe that you know what is best for you. Always trust yourself.

Cornerstones to This Book

a) Allow new ideas to linger as a 'maybe', and keep adding to these new ideas through other books and information, because this increases your willingness to try new ideas. Consider all information as a launching pad that builds bridges to even more amazing knowledge and greater understanding. There is never a need to decide whether an idea is 'in or out'.

b) Experiment with new ideas, as this gives you greater understanding and demonstrates the power of the concept.

c) It is vital that you are honest with yourself throughout this book. Some of these concepts may challenge you, and that's okay. You will only grow when you are ready to see yourself for who you are.

d) Read and enjoy this book with a light heart and make laughter a priority everyday. Laughter is a natural high for all of us. Consciously choose to laugh rather than accept the seriousness of daily life.

When You Are Ready

This book always teaches you at your level, because you will pick up ideas when you are ready to discover. At all times, remember it is best to grow at your own pace. This powerful information works its own magic to get you started without your even realizing it. When you are ready to grow, change or consider new ideas, you will always be in the perfect place to do so, and you will have all the motivation you need. No matter what the subject in this book, if you are inspired by an idea, explore it, but if not, then leave it and move on to the next section.

Firstly, I discuss who you really are, so you can grasp the full extent of your inner power. Then, I discuss the importance of loving yourself, and why you are entitled to live the most brilliant life imaginable. Six sections follow.

Section 1 – Your purpose for being on Earth.

Section 2 – Taking responsibility for your life and how doing that gets you what you want.

Section 3 – Paving the way. What to attend to, so you can get what you want.

Section 4 – Creating what you want. Taking what you have learnt and creating your brilliant life. This includes components that speed up the realization of your dreams.

Section 5 – Other people and how they affect your ability to get what you want.

Section 6 – How to stay focused every day on what you want.

At the end of each chapter, I summarize the chapter into several points. You may choose one or two points to reflect on and to introduce into your life.

Let's Pause for a Moment…
…and make this as easy as possible.

The Adventure Is in Your Mind

You learn best when you are feeling loved, energized and motivated to change and grow, therefore it's essential to put yourself in an environment where you feel fabulous. You want to be as happy and open to new potentials as possible, inspired to discover how to get anything you want.

So, work with me now…and dive into this.

Imagine you're on an exciting adventure, being transported to a spectacular place deep within…a place where you walk tall, feel treasured, glow with warmth, feel embraced by love, and every particle in your being dances with happiness. A vivid rainbow of magnificent colours fills your being with possibility, harmony and peace. Here in this magical place you've always welcomed new ideas and you've always been lovingly honest with yourself. You're a powerful person who takes action, and you make your dreams come true.

In your mind, tick each box before proceeding:
☐ I am entitled to a brilliant life.
☐ I am energized by and drawn toward new ideas.
☐ I am honest with myself and enthusiastically seek opportunities to learn about myself.
☐ I am an action person who makes my own dreams come true.
☐ I actively seek laughter everyday, lots of it.

Transport yourself to your special place each time you read this book. You'll feel cherished, open and inspired to learn and grow.

Journal Your Journey

Consider having a special journal on hand for some of the exercises in this book. It's also an ideal place to keep ideas and insights. Buying a special journal is a way of telling yourself you are taking action.

Who Are You Really?

"You don't have a soul. You are a soul. You have a body."

C.S. Lewis

(Author, Chronicles of Narnia, 1898–1963)

*I*f you want to change your life and get what you want, you'll need fresh new ways of thinking. Celebrate! You're about to give yourself a spectacular gift of new knowledge. I offer you easy, fabulous, powerful potentials, and if they resonate, even slightly, allow yourself to explore the ideas. Most of us feel safer with absolute conclusions about life, but these block us from further discovery. Keep everything you learn, anywhere, anytime, as a possibility until you have experienced it. Shake yourself free.

How do your thoughts affect your life? To understand this, first you need to understand who you really are, and for that we need to clarify the source of *your power*. Once you awaken and acknowledge the power within you, you will harness it to create any life you choose. You can still create a brilliant life without exploring the source of your power; however, with this knowledge, you'll glide into understanding how you create your life, collecting greater empowerment and freedom along the way. If any of the concepts are a challenge for you to consider, feel free to skip to the next chapter and read on from there, because you'll still be on track to create your brilliant life.

You Are Your Own Personal Power

It's widely acknowledged that when someone dies, their Spirit or soul exits the body. The Spirit within each of us is another word for the God-consciousness or God-force within each of us – the life force in everything. This is our 'intelligence' – the consciousness that gives us life.

Many people have reached this point of understanding, however they rarely consider that if everyone has this God-consciousness, and if God is in everything, then it follows that each of us has God within us.

Let's play with that idea. We are all Gods, created from God. We come directly from the source of all life.[2] God is you, and you are a God. For some people, this may seem inconceivable, but allow the concept to linger…and try it on. Actually, when I first heard the idea of being a God, it instantly resonated with me, and I immediately investigated further.[3] It was completely new to me, but after all the studies I had done, it made the most sense, and since then I have been creating even more in my life by exploring it and trying it out. This is also how I discovered a link with quantum physics, which we'll get to in the coming pages.

Some people have chosen to completely discard the idea of God, and some have been taught that God is to be feared. Some feel that God is separate, and outside of them, while for others identifying with being a God is close to sacrilege. Each of us has our own unique perception of God, but it's probably true to say that many people would struggle to feel worthy of being a God.

It's much simpler and easier to take charge of your life when you know the power is *within* you, rather than *outside* of you and beyond your control. The God within you *is* your power, and is gentle, loving and completely accepting. Your God within takes every one of your thoughts in every moment and uses them to create your life in every moment. What you think creates your world, and you are the one who chooses every thought. Once you know this, there is nothing haphazard about your life any more. You are your own power…you decide and control your life. You have free will to live your life in any way you choose, and your choices are never judged…they are never considered to be right or wrong. Your God creates your life unquestioningly…according to your thoughts. You are able to choose any life, behave in any way, and never be judged by your God within.

Does this sound slightly different? Okay...it's radically different from what most of us were always taught.

You are free to think anything you like or change your mind in any moment. You are always loved. You are free to accept or deny any thought or idea. Until now, many people have chosen anxiety, misery, hatred, addiction and disease, but if they are prepared to open their minds to a power source within them, they can instantly choose to change all that...simply using their thoughts, without needing help from anyone or any other being.

If this is true it sounds amazing, doesn't it? What a way to live! It seems incredible...no right and wrong, never judged, loved always, choosing any life, getting anything you want...phew! But this *is* real; it's all yours to keep.

You Become Instantly More Loving

When you start to consider the idea of being a God, you may feel awkward and concerned that you'll become arrogant. Instead, it is a quiet, humble self-realization, which you can keep to yourself. When you grasp the understanding of being a God, instead of flaunting it you immediately become more loving, compassionate, patient, understanding, accepting and modest. In addition, you'll also experience a freeing and incomparable sense of power and purpose. You'll realize, too, that everyone else is also a God, so we are all the same: we all have equal potential.

Everyone is Free

If we all genuinely considered ourselves to be Gods, we'd have overwhelming love and peace in the world. I say 'genuinely' because there can be an instinctive fear of this power being abused, of people becoming tyrants. If we truly understood this concept, then we would not need to take power from someone else. Everyone would feel free, secure and happy with this power.

So Where's the Proof?

Constantly demanding proof can be a stumbling block in our spiritual growth, but fortunately, in this case quantum physics comes to the rescue. It is only fairly recently that quantum physics gained sufficient acceptance to dismantle the traditional laws of biochemistry and physics. Sometimes the truth is hard to prove, and pioneering quantum physicists had to face serious hostilities from traditional scientists, who were concerned about their credibility and wanted the old ways to stay, despite undeniable proof to the contrary.[1] This science proves that we hold the power to create our world. This science shows us how we live. This science *is* our life.

All matter – everything you can see and touch – is made up of subatomic particles. Scientists have found that the subatomic world consists of energy waves. These energy waves contain within them everything anyone could possibly want in this world. What you want starts out *in* these waves of energy. These waves exist with all potentials until the moment someone looks at them. The act of observing the waves chooses one possibility or outcome and locks it down to a single state. Scientists discovered this when various researchers encountered different results from the same experiment, and realized it was the *thought* of whichever scientist doing the 'observing' that decided which single possibility or outcome would be the result. Without realizing it, every day, through your thoughts, you are 'observing' these energy waves and making choices. Those choices become your reality. Quantum physicists have called this the Observer Effect, and this is where *you* enter the world of quantum physics.

Every situation you face every day, every thought you have, is like a quantum physics experiment. Quantum physicists found that whatever you, the Observer, *think* will happen in your life *is* what happens. In every moment, you are having a thought, and this means that in every moment you are choosing a specific potential from the quantum world and locking down that choice to become your own unique reality in the moment. Change your thought, and in a flash you land in a different reality. Your thoughts choose your reality; your life is decided by *you*.[1, 4]

Let's review for a moment. Whatever you *think* will happen… *is* what happens. *You* are the power source in your world – this is now proven by science!

If quantum physics is new to you, this may sound crazy. Hopefully, it's a fascinating kind of crazy. I have barely scratched the surface in my explanation, but there are many books available that further explain quantum physics in an easy manner (see Appendix B). Gaining a better understanding of *how* your thoughts become the life you live helps you get anything you want. Further study heightens your understanding and acceptance, and you are more likely to try it. The bottom line is that quantum physics simplifies life tremendously. It helps you grasp the concept of how you have created your entire life, how you got to be where you are today and how you can consciously change your future. When you hold this key, you can create anything. Bring it on!

> *"Do not believe in anything simply because you have heard it. Do not believe in anything simply because it is spoken and rumoured by many. Do not believe in anything simply because it is found written in your religious books. Do not believe in anything merely on the authority of your teachers and elders. Do not believe in traditions because they have been handed down for many generations. But after observation and analysis, when you find that anything agrees with reason and is conducive to the good and benefit of one and all, then accept it and live up to it."*

> Buddha
> (Spiritual teacher and founder of Buddhism, 563–483 BC)

Past Lives and Your Body

You've probably already heard about the concept of past lives, but perhaps you're unsure what to make of it. Actually, this notion makes little difference to your ability to create a magnificent life. I mention it so as to add to your freedom and perspective by explaining that each lifetime, you arrive in a new body, which means you are eternal. If the body dies, *you* the Spirit live on eternally. Eternally? Yes, this means you're free *right now*, because *you* live forever.[3, 5] You can do a little dance if you want to.

When we are ready for fresh ways of thinking, some concepts may require us to loosen up, trust our inner knowing and be ready to investigate further. There is so much more to us than we know. It's easy to get caught up in our daily lives and forget that our planet is only a tiny dot in the Milky Way, and that it is estimated that in that galaxy alone are billions of suns, other planets and certainly more life. If you can open your mind to imagine the magnitude of all this, it instantly takes you to the realization that there will always be more to learn.

So, here you are; a Spirit having a human experience. And what do you need for a human experience? Right. A body... which means that your body is only something you reside in to experience life on Earth; that is all. You are not, in essence, your body. Therefore, although your body is precious, and you should take care of it and appreciate it, avoid identifying too closely with it. Your body has no interest in the Spirit who gives it life. Your body's prime focus is avoiding death. It feels that the best way to ensure survival is by being overly cautious and by staying well clear of new ideas.

> *"I can't explain myself, I'm afraid, because I'm not myself,*
> *you see." Alice.*
>
> Lewis Carroll
> (Author, Alice's Adventures in Wonderland,
> 1832–1898)

A new idea usually rings alarm bells in the body because changing or shifting to a new way of living means saying goodbye to the way it used to be. To the body, goodbye is the same as death, so the body says, 'I will do whatever I can to avoid new ideas...I hate changing, I can't predict the outcome – new ideas threaten my survival.' The body only focuses on its immediate needs. 'Keep my life the same, keep me warm and fed and I will be happy.' What a deception! Survival mode is *boring* at best, and creates an overwhelming sense of being without purpose.

> *"If we don't change we don't grow. If we don't grow we are*
> *not really living."*
>
> Gail Sheehy
> (American author and writer, b. 1937)

On top of all this, the body is preoccupied with how it looks and what others think, and it competes to demonstrate intellect, success and wealth. It is unsettled, and constantly gathers more material items to feel better or look good, but it never quite feels sufficiently safe or satisfied, so it can never stop its feverish gathering. No wonder this creates so much anxiety, illness and confusion, not to mention anger, impatience and frustration. There is no lasting peace and happiness to be found in looking good, having material items or beating others to the finish line. What to do?

Your Soul Tells You What to Do

This is where your soul enters the mix. It holds a special place, and it is there to record all your thoughts, experiences, emotions and the wisdom you gain. Your soul is your eternal memory and your conscience, encouraging you to move on from continually repeating the same experiences. When you learn how to listen, you'll find your soul uses special inner urges that show you exactly what new experiences you should pursue, so as to gain new understandings about life, achieve greater wisdom and happiness, and get what you want. How do you recognize an inner urge? It's when you are keen to try something that makes you feel excited and happy, and brings you joy and delight. You could perhaps feel slightly nervous about it, but something tells you that you want to do it. You may even find that your urges do not seem logical, and you will discover the reason for this later. When you do what makes you happy, you are following your inner urges; you are following your soul and you are mastering your body. If you are no longer happy, or you feel bored, you'll get an inner urge to finish what you are doing and change to something new. This means your soul is finished with this experience. To stay happy, you need to move on to something else. This can happen in your career, relationships, or any other area of your life. You must gain new experiences to ensure fulfilment, otherwise you get bored, grumpy, frustrated.[3]

Mastering Your Body

"The world hates change but it is the only thing that has brought progress."

Charles F Kettering
(American engineer and inventor of the electric starter motor, who held 140 patents and owned the company Delco, later sold to General Motors, 1876–1958)

Your God within is all-knowing, wise, infinite and abundant, and it keeps your body safer than the body could ever do by itself.[3] Mastering the body takes skill and persistence because the body likes being in control so it can minimize changes and keep a firm grip on its 'safe' future. If you are determined enough to submit yourself to change, your body develops flexibility in handling it. It may still be a little nervous, but it steadily becomes more open to new ideas and more adaptable. As you open the door a little more for the real you, you start to master your body, and your body in turn gradually trusts being guided or controlled. Then, you get more of what you want.

As an example, ATMs (automatic teller machines) seem like they've been around forever, but when they were introduced in the 1980s many people avoided them as if they had a strange aura about them. People created reasons for staying clear of ATMs, worrying that they would swallow their card, or they may get stuck during the process. Once they had used a machine, however, they understood their smooth ease and practicality, and loved them.

Most people let their body run their life, instead of listening to their soul. When you listen to your soul, you deliberately create powerful thoughts for your God to follow. You gradually reduce the body's dominance by becoming more attentive to your thoughts, releasing your unwanted emotions, and learning to love yourself in every moment. Some people call this 'the journey'. It is a journey to gradually master your body, to listen to your soul and to accept and love yourself more and more along the way. It becomes a straight line to happiness, greater wisdom and living your magical life.

Your ideal path is a deep inner knowing from your soul. When you are ready to listen to your soul, everything changes. You become aligned with the true path for you, and your body transforms, becoming like that of a child that has gained guidance and direction, until finally it relaxes…all that anxiety, illness, confusion, anger and impatience magically vanish, and you have harmony. You get more of what you want. You get the material items you want, as well as peace, love, happiness and fulfilment.

By staying determined, the balance eventually tips in favour of your Spirit and soul. You find yourself spontaneously following your soul's desires and actively searching for experiences that lift your attitudes, allow greater thoughts and enable happiness every day. The greater your thoughts, the more fun you have every day. While you still need to put in some mental effort, your thoughts and actions more easily align with your soul's wisdom. You also gain a new level of fulfilment.

When You Realize Who You Are

Many of us have been told that we must work through angels, Jesus, Buddha and so on, to create our dreams. It is common to hear people say, 'Well, you're only human.' In fact, Earth may only be a little dot in the Milky Way, but you are every bit as powerful as any being in any universe when you are on the ideal path for you, and if you are open to any possibility. You are capable of the miraculous; let that be your potential.

Think deliberately and consciously so as to give your God the freedom to create the marvellous. Once you have the appropriate knowledge, it is much easier. You can take it one step at a time, one day at a time, and do it when you are ready – in your own time.

Once you realize who you really are, you have the power to create the life you want – and everyone in your life benefits. It is powerful knowing that life doesn't happen to you haphazardly, and that your future is secure.

The wonderful aspect about your growth is that you do not have to wait for someone else to change, or for them to help you. You do it all yourself, and everything you need is already within you. You have it all...you *always* had it all.

Summary of

"Who Are You Really?"

♦   If you want to change your life, you'll need new ways of thinking.

- Keep an open mind, resist the need for absolute conclusions and keep everything as a potential.
- Consider the concept of God being within you.
- You cannot truly take charge of your life until you start to appreciate the power you already have within you.
- You have free will to live your life as you choose.
- You are the Observer in your life according to quantum physics, and whatever you think will happen is what happens.
- Your body is really clothing for your God within, and your body's main focus is survival.
- Your Spirit, God or Observer is the real you. This is who should run your life. Your body should be cherished and cared for, but it should not run your life.
- Your soul knows what experiences you need in order to evolve. It propels you to create new experiences that help you grow, and it leads you to happiness and getting what you want.
- One of your goals on Earth is to master your body by listening to your soul.
- Master your body by becoming aware of your thoughts, by understanding and releasing your unwanted emotions, and by learning to love yourself.
- Allowing your God within to run your life enables you to create your ideal life.
- You are every bit as powerful as any being in the universe.
- You are capable of the miraculous – choose that as your potential.
- You do not have to wait for someone else to change or for them to help you. You do it yourself.

Section 1

The Reason You Are On Earth

"Happiness is the meaning and purpose of life, the whole aim and end of human existence."

Aristotle

(Ancient Greek philosopher, scientist, physician, 384–322 BC)

*Y*ou do have a purpose here. Actually you have several purposes. You have come to Earth to experience life on this planet, and your main purposes are to achieve a continuous state of happiness and to expand your wisdom. It's true, you're meant to be happy! This is what we mean by evolving or growing. Another purpose for being on Earth, as mentioned earlier, is to create new experiences. These urgings come from your soul – it knows what's good for you. Think about it – when you want something and get it, it means you'll have a new experience. In other words, it doesn't make sense that you'd be yearning for aspects of your life that you've already got or always had.

The springboard to taking action and using the opportunities presented to you by your soul starts with learning to love yourself and being willing to learn about both yourself and life in general. You are unlikely to get what you truly want without continually adding to your knowledge and taking steps to increase your love for yourself. This is because if you are stuck in a repetitive, unloving, frustrating life relying on the same knowledge you've had for years, the body can trick you into wanting things that are *empty* for you, that will feel good for only five minutes. The body doesn't listen to the soul – *you* do. You need to *wake up* and live life to the full. It's a magical life out there, so go out and get it. This is all explained in the pages that follow.

CHAPTER 1

Loving Yourself Is Essential

"Love yourself first and everything falls into line."

Lucille Ball
(American radio and motion picture actress
and comedy star, 1911–1989)

The moment you choose to start loving yourself, you instantly enjoy greater freedom and naturally start choosing the best life for you.

Loving yourself is the first step on your journey toward greater wisdom, happiness and what you want. No matter what your current circumstances, *create an intention now* to love yourself more every day. Make it a mission to completely approve of everything you have ever said or done. Right now, you hold this essential key to your happy life.

How Important Do You Think You Are?

Your inner power, freedom and happiness, and whether you are living the life you want, are directly connected to how much you love yourself. This is because if you want to grow, you need to consider yourself worth the investment.

Self-love can be a confusing concept, depending on your childhood experiences. If you were told to put others first, you probably think others are more important. Most children know intuitively that they are just as important, which probably prompted an internal struggle for you. Additionally, parents may criticize their children's work, abilities or personality, thereby sending their children messages that they are not good enough. Children need to know that they are loved exactly the way they are, and need to be encouraged to love themselves first.

Some people appear to love themselves because they buy expensive items and go on glorious holidays. Frequently, these are bought in an effort to feel worthwhile. Other people appear to love themselves because they behave in an arrogant, self-important, haughty manner. This, of course, repels most people. There is a humility that goes with loving yourself, and an inner peace that requires nothing outside of you.

"If you aren't good at loving yourself, you will have a difficult time loving anyone, since you'll resent the time and energy you give another person that you aren't even giving to yourself."

Barbara De Angelis
(American researcher on relationships and personal growth)

When You Put Yourself First, You'll Love Others

Then there are other people who think loving themselves is to the detriment of others. The reverse is true. Truly loving yourself, and putting yourself first, is hugely beneficial to others. Loving yourself merges your love with others. When your 'love tank' is full and you allow yourself to be the most important person in your life, you gain the most wonderful ability and freedom to love others beyond your imagination. There ceases to be a separation; instead, you have the deepest connection.

Initially you may need courage to do this, as it seems 'selfish', but that is simply the conditioning you've had. Be brave, and do it anyway. The safety instructions on board any airline say to firstly apply your own oxygen mask and then assist others. This isn't selfish, it is sensible. Take care of you first and you'll have even more time for others. Each time you truly love yourself to a greater extent, you will notice a leap in your love and acceptance of others. When this happens, it's almost impossible to describe – it is so rewarding, beautiful and amazing, so powerful.

Try this: look in a mirror and say, 'I am precious, special and amazing.' Notice if this is a challenge for you. Never mind how strange this seems – you may need to pretend you mean it at first, but say it with conviction. Your entire body will naturally glow upon hearing it. Fill your body with a beautiful warmth, and keep saying it until you feel a subtle change, like a tingling sensation, in your body. This means you have increased your vibration, and the higher your vibration, the happier you are. Your body will eagerly join in to play, even when you are pretending. Keep saying that, or something similarly sensational, throughout the day, every day. Each time you say it, you are training your brain for self-love. Your love for yourself becomes more radiant every time.

Once you achieve that warm glow from showing yourself love, notice how much more powerful you feel. Make it a priority to love yourself every day. No more criticizing yourself, no more finding fault with your body, no more groaning about your past, what someone else did to you or what might have been.

I was at a seminar doing a technique designed to help master my body. I had high expectations about my performance, but I wasn't achieving the results I wanted. Needless to say, I was having a frustrating time and becoming hugely disappointed with myself. With a jolt, I suddenly recognized I was viciously attacking myself by saying I wasn't good enough, that I wasn't trying hard enough – I was saying things I'd never say to anyone else. I was appalled.

Once I figured out what I was doing, I changed my approach and spent a few minutes calming myself, telling myself how wonderful and special I am. As I continued the exercise, I continued to be gentle, encouraging and loving with myself, even if I didn't achieve the results I wanted. The transformation was immediate and overwhelming. I felt a wave of beautiful love wash over me.

In this moment, I finally comprehended the beauty of accepting and loving myself despite my results. That pure, sweet feeling was freedom to me and a crystallization of everything I had worked for so far in life. No material item could match that beautiful, euphoric feeling. I was astonished at the wonderfulness of the feeling, especially as it was self-created (we're so used to needing others to make us feel good). I had done the incredible and made myself feel happier than anyone else ever could. I felt truly powerful.

On top of that, I also understood that loving myself was more important than exceptional performance. In fact, I found the more I loved myself the more I excelled. I had been putting the cart before the horse.

Love is Irresistible and it is Free

Love is essential for a fulfilled life. Subconsciously, everyone seeks love, and we all radiate warmth and joy when we feel loved. It is one of the most powerful forces in the universe. It is free, and the more you give out, the more you get back. It is fundamental to living your great life. It also affects your relationship with others in the following ways:

- You are only capable of loving others to the extent you love yourself.
- You will only attract as much love into your life as you give to yourself.
- The less you love yourself, the more unlikely it is that you will find love in a relationship.
- When you love yourself enough, you do not need love from others, and yet you will receive an abundance.

When you focus on loving yourself you'll get results, just as you get results when you focus and spend time on a project at work. Allow only supportive and encouraging thoughts about yourself, and each day it becomes easier.

You're Always Worth it

No matter what you have ever done, you are worthy of love and getting what you want. Everything you do is so you can gain experience, learn, understand life and develop wisdom.[3] This moment, *now*, is fresh and pure, and your past is gone. In every situation, you are doing the best you can at the time. Certainly, you can always do better, but in every moment you do your best. Doing your best should always be good enough. Guilt was never meant to be a part of your life – guilt was something the body took on.

If you feel guilty because of your actions and it continues on for too long, you're likely to move into apathy, frustration or depression, which creates more problems, not only for yourself, but for those around you, too. Guilt is of no value to anyone. Give guilt the boot, and strike it out of your life forever.

> *"The more anger towards the past you carry in your heart,*
> *the less capable you are of loving in the present."*
>
> Barbara De Angelis
> (American researcher on relationships and personal growth)

So You're Not Perfect

Believe it or not, the goal is not perfection. What is perfection, anyway? How can there be perfection? Imagine how boring life would be with perfection.[3] We are fortunate that there is always more to learn, and that life keeps changing.

Many of us are in a holding pattern until we feel perfect enough to love ourselves and have what we want. You are always improving. View it that way, and you'll find the more you love yourself, the more perfect you'll become. As an alternative goal, decide to make each day the best you have ever lived. By loving yourself as you are, you are both happier and healthier. The power of loving yourself dissolves disease. It is hugely empowering to love yourself as you are, and to realize you have always done your best.

The Blessings of Your Past

Always gain wisdom by learning from every situation, but move on. The more you can leave your past behind and be happy in this moment, the happier you are and so is everyone around you.

You are greater today because of your past. You have more wisdom because of your past. Regardless of your past, only your thoughts right now matter. Today, you are always in the best place to make changes and to have what you want. Not yesterday, not tomorrow…today.

Everything starts with choosing to love yourself, choosing to make an investment in yourself and feeling entitled to get what you want.

When you love yourself, you are drawn to actively explore all that life has to offer…and to *explore* is why you are here. Love inspires learning. Love provides freedom for you, and pulls you toward new discoveries and experiences. Your love lifts you up. You feel outrageous, confident and secure, capable of achieving anything.

Choose to be inspired and vibrant today. Create your magnificent life *today* – live it today.

From here on, magic happens. Once you love yourself you are truly loved. And when you are loved, you can achieve anything.

Summary of

"Loving Yourself is Essential"

- ◆ The more you love yourself, the greater the life you create.
- ◆ Loving yourself benefits others.
- ◆ Courageously love yourself first, and find that there is a flow-on effect for everyone.
- ◆ Consider yourself worth the investment. Every moment you invest in yourself helps you and everyone else.
- ◆ Being kind and loving to yourself is an essential first step toward a fulfilled life.
- ◆ Say something sensational about yourself every time you look in the mirror.
- ◆ No matter what you have ever done, you are worthy of love.
- ◆ We are not perfect, and the goal is not perfection. Continued discovery, learning and new experiences keep us fulfilled.
- ◆ Guilt is of no value to anyone. The more you focus on creating a magnificent life, the less guilt you encounter.
- ◆ You are greater today because of your past. Keep the wisdom and leave the past behind.
- ◆ Only your thoughts right now matter.

♦ When you love yourself, you naturally want to learn more about life and explore. Love gives you the freedom and the confidence to do this.

EXERCISE: How to Love Yourself More

1. As you look in the mirror while brushing your teeth, use the time to praise every aspect of yourself, even those aspects you consider need to change. Acknowledge that you always do your best, and your best is good enough for you.

2. Through the day, practice saying inspiring and empowering things about yourself and to others. Affirmations are a great way to inspire yourself, and keep you present and focused, and are covered in more detail at the end of this book in Section 6 *The Gift of Every New Day*. Have some fun by writing down several inspirational things about yourself. Place them in a few places around your house – next to your bed, in the pantry, next to your computer, and so on. For example:

♦ I give myself all the love I need and want.
♦ I love myself first and foremost.
♦ I find it easy to say loving things to myself every day.
♦ I remember to say loving things to myself every day.
♦ I get satisfaction saying loving things to myself.
♦ I think I am fabulous. I am fabulous.
♦ I acknowledge that I always do my best.
♦ I feel safe, confident and secure in myself. I am enough.
♦ I am motivated to learn more about myself and to live a fabulous life.
♦ I do whatever it takes to live a wonderful life.
♦ I grow every day and I am worth the investment.

3. Contemplate the things you love doing and what stops you from doing them. Make a date to do some of them, or at least start to take action toward doing them. When you do them,

mark the occasion. Life should be fun, so celebrate when you allow yourself to be happy.

4. Catch yourself speaking about yourself – notice what words you use.

5. If you notice something critical about yourself, replace it with something that makes you feel great. Congratulate yourself for being aware enough to notice. It is this awareness that will ultimately be your friend.

6. As you go to sleep at night, reflect on your wonderful attributes, and those you've recently added. Express gratitude for your day and your life.

7. Congratulate yourself every time you have uplifting thoughts about yourself and about life.

CHAPTER 2

Getting To
What You Want
and Beyond

*"The human Spirit needs to accomplish, achieve, to triumph,
to be happy."*

Ben Stein, b. 1944
(American attorney, political figure, entertainment personality and
speechwriter for U.S. Presidents Nixon and Ford)

We've talked about one fundamental element to getting what you want – *loving yourself*. Now let's move even closer to what you want and discuss the other element – *new knowledge*.

The more you *learn* about yourself and life, the more you'll *love* yourself, and subsequently…the more you *love* yourself, the greater your passion for *learning*.

These two elements are essential, for it is from them that *happiness* is ignited and introduced into the mix, which leads you directly to getting what you want.

New Knowledge Builds Your Acceptance to
Get What You Want

Constant learning is essential to your happiness. Your soul tells you what the ideal knowledge and experiences are for you.

It urges you in that direction. If you follow the urges, they put you in a desirable position from which to expand your insights about yourself and life. Discovering new knowledge is stimulating and inspirational. Books and courses open your mind to possibilities in your life. The more you know about a subject, the less mystery there is; you have less fear, and you are more likely to sign up and give it a go. Knowledge builds your ability to accept that you can get what you want – therefore it is easier to get what you want. The more you accept the power of a concept, the better your outcome.[3, 4]

The body also becomes more open to the information, because it has seen it or heard of it before. It's similar to advertising, whereby people are more likely to buy a well-branded product than one they have never heard of. It somehow feels safer.

"There is a great difference between knowing and understanding: you can know a lot about something and not really understand it."

Charles F Kettering
(American engineer and inventor of the electric starter motor, who held 140 patents and owned the company Delco, later sold to General Motors, 1876–1958)

New Experiences Keep You Growing

Once you've been drawn to learning about new ideas, take the next step and apply them in your life. While the knowledge adds to your acceptance levels, new experiences keep you growing, and drive you toward what you want in life. They teach you about both yourself and life. The combination of new knowledge and experience forms wisdom.[3] Greater awareness is part of the wisdom you gain. You have a wonderful sense of being observant, you are more objective and you start sensing that you can be more powerful than any situation. You are able to notice your thoughts in the moment, as well as what is happening around you.

It's Scientific: New Knowledge + Experience = Happiness

The science of neuroplasticity, which is explained in the coming pages, has found strong evidence as to why new knowledge and experiences keep us healthy and happy.

It seems that *new* mental activities – preferably ones we enjoy – keep our brain younger by maintaining our ability to pay attention and to learn new information. Endlessly repeating the same activities, even crossword puzzles, causes us to lose those abilities.

There also seems to be a link between the state of our happiness and how many new neurons we produce. They apparently help us to see the world in new and different ways, and to recognize when we are having new experiences. If our world looks the same every day, it's depressing. Scientists have found that physical exercise, e.g. walking, stimulates the production of new neurons, mainly through increased oxygen supply to the brain, but have noted that more of these new neurons survive if they're supported by stimulating new mental activities. Without physical exercise and new experiences, the brain atrophies.[6, 7]

Only Do What *You* Love

Follow paths that captivate you, as opposed to what your family and friends expect. Do what you want to. Listen to your inner compass. When you satisfy an interest, or accomplish as much as you can from undertaking an experience, search again for something new. Once you've mastered something, move on. Learning keeps you inspired and happy.

> "If you put yourself in a position where you have to stretch outside your comfort zone, then you are forced to expand your consciousness."
>
> Les Brown
> (American author, entrepreneur and motivational speaker)

Keep gently stretching your comfort zone. Make sure there is a sense of fun and challenge in most of what you do. Your soul is drawn to challenges; it finds them fun. The body can be a little afraid of change and something different, but when you've jumped that hurdle, you feel liberated, powerful and inspired.

Initially, you may be unsure of what new experiences you need, but as you gather knowledge and allow access to that place of deep inner knowing, you gain insight. You have probably lived countless lives before this one.[3, 5] Living on Earth right now, no matter what your situation, with this information you have a golden opportunity to make this life your best ever. All the information required for your growth is readily available in this life if you want it and choose to find it.

"The purpose of our lives is to be happy."

Dalai Lama

(Head of the Gelugpa order of Tibetan buddhists, awarded the 1989 Nobel Peace Prize, b. 1935)

Creating... Gets You What You Want

Goals are vital to ensure your growth toward wisdom, happiness and what you want. When you create goals or focus on a special dream, you are intentionally setting up new opportunities for more learning and life experience. Your soul loves to dream and to create. Without challenges and new experiences, life is dull, and seems to stand still, causing frustration.

Creating is easy and inspiring – it is merely making, learning or trying anything new to you. Just as painting a beautiful picture is being creative, so is taking a course, trying a new way of thinking, painting your house a different colour or dreaming of a new goal. There are numerous opportunities to be creative in your life every day. Use them to give this life every opportunity to be the greatest. Start listening to your soul, and do what you truly want to do.

Material items also play a part in creating new experiences. You are drawn to these if you need to experience them. They may not bring lasting happiness, but if you can generate them in your life that's magical, because it means you can create anything in your life in the same way.

"All truths are easy to understand once they are discovered; the point is to discover them."

Galileo Galilei

(1564–1642)

Knowing the Truth... Gets You What You Want

When you get the feeling you've finally 'got' something, it is immensely satisfying, but it only arrives when you have tried out what you have learnt. Experience leads to an integral understanding about the knowledge you have gathered, and you then know whether it is true or not. The experience you gain means you can go beyond the need to 'believe'. You are the one who discovers what is true for you. Your experience is unique, as is your truth. Everyone's version of the truth is different, because everyone's knowledge and experience is different. Until you reach this point, you may still doubt the information, because you haven't lived it. Your understanding of the truth is always building and expanding…you are always evolving, and it is only *your* experience that matters.[3, 5]

For many years, I was fascinated by the link between nutrition and health, and the effects of vitamins, minerals, aromatherapy etc., on the body. More information kept coming to light, which I avidly studied. I tried a few nutritional methods such as Fit for Life (food combining), The Zone, and Eat Right for Your (Blood) Type. Each one made sense and worked for me, added a piece to the puzzle, and was 'true' for me at the time, but I was always open to more learning. Eventually, I evolved to understand that it is ultimately my attitude that determines my health, and not what I eat. If we are sad and disgruntled about life, our body reflects that, whereas the happier we are, the healthier we are. Additionally, if we believe something is unhealthy, it is. As might be expected, the more you dislike yourself or feel sad, the more likely food is to be unhealthy in your body.

I loved the discovery aspect of each step, and my wisdom blossomed with each new understanding. However, as a truth unfolds for us, we must be mindful of the need to continue gathering experience to enable more complete understanding. In a case such as this, as the truth unfolds, continue with a 'healthy' diet until your understanding evolves to a state where you can eat anything and be stronger and healthier than ever.

"We don't receive wisdom; we must discover it for ourselves after a journey that no one can take for us or spare us."

Marcel Proust
(French novelist, 1871–1922)

Wisdom... Gets You What You Want

Your collection of knowledge, along with your exploration and active participation in life, puts you on a direct escalating path toward greater wisdom. The more you understand about yourself and life, the greater your wisdom. Each day is approached with joy and anticipation of the wonderful. Each day becomes filled with more happiness, fulfilment and freedom. The benefits are infinite.

One of the advantages of wisdom is that it increases your common sense and intuition, and gives you the courage to use it, thereby granting you what you want. If someone values intellectual knowledge over wisdom, they are jeopardizing their common sense and intuition. This sometimes happens in societies where intellectual knowledge means success and prestige. This is limiting, as it means the body is making decisions without accessing the wisdom that is readily available in the soul.

Wisdom also creates the desire to further understand the nuances of life:

- Getting closer to the truth becomes more important than holding on to your current views.
- Your mind is wide open. You love considering and trying new information.
- You are flexible and quickly adapt to new situations.
- You acquire a concern for the well-being of everyone around you.
- You have freedom to make independent decisions, and your decisions are loving, mature, ethical and sensible.
- You have the ability to anticipate and avoid potential problems and conflict.
- Gratitude becomes a sparkling integral part of your day.
- You have a rational approach to life.
- You know how to face situations calmly, with purpose and compassion.
- Life is seen from a higher perspective and you instinctively consider other points of view.
- You are also able to determine when doing nothing is the best option.

The following diagram outlines the pathway from knowledge to happiness and getting what you want. Note that every stage helps you get what you want, however it becomes easier once you reach a state of happiness.

Knowledge	Providing new insights into your potentials and building acceptance.
Action	Choosing to apply the knowledge to your life.
Experience	Living the knowledge.
Truth	The result of your experience – your unique integral understanding about the knowledge.
Wisdom	An eternal gift – a knowingness, your ability to understand the bigger picture, to make independent decisions and get what you want faster.
Happiness	Increased power, confidence, freedom and choice in your life.
What You Want	Celebrate!

As you gain more clarity about your purpose, you will start to notice more about what you are doing on Earth. A simple walk in a forest will take on new meaning, as you comprehend that you are a Spirit in a body. Touching and feeling a leaf suddenly becomes a cherished moment – you feel the leaf with elation and clarity. Once you crystallize a moment like this, you gain tremendous gratitude and your life takes on a new vitality and purpose.

Growth becomes essential to your day because every day adds to life's magnificence and to your achievement and satisfaction. Your brilliant new awareness, truth and wisdom solidify in you, and you then build on them.

> *"Nothing is worth more than this day."*
>
> Johann Wolfgang von Goethe
> (German writer 1749–1832)

Now Is All There Ever Is...Dive into What You Want Now

Today is the ideal moment to use your knowledge and act on opportunities. Now is the only moment you can ever take action. Any time you are ready will be *now* for you, and you have endless opportunities to seize your moment to act. Remember, however, that constantly postponing action leaves your brilliant life forever in the future.

Once you are on a path of learning, discovery and new experiences, you are gaining wisdom. You are heading in the ideal direction for happiness and for getting anything you want. And you are on your way to fulfilling your purpose in coming to Earth.

Summary of

"Getting to What You Want and Beyond"

♦ The urges from your soul lead you to ideal knowledge and experiences, tailored to you.

♦ Constant learning is vital for keeping you on a path to happiness.

- The happier you are, the more you will get what you want.
- Keep learning, as this removes mystery and fear.
- The more you learn, the more you accept the fact that you can get what you want; therefore, it is easier to get what you want.
- While learning is important, so is trying out the knowledge. Otherwise, it remains just a good idea.
- Experience leads to an integral understanding about new knowledge, and you then know whether it is true or not. You are the one who discovers what is true for you. Everyone's version of the truth is different.
- Your soul loves to dream and create. Actively look for ways to learn, make or try something new.
- Trying something new, such as a new activity, provides new information, understanding and awareness.
- Try different interests and concepts. Doing the same activities every day produces boredom and frustration. Stretch your comfort zone.
- Follow your inner compass when deciding your direction. Do what you want to do rather than what family and friends think.
- Choose this opportunity on Earth to make this your best life ever.
- Creating goals sets up opportunities for more wisdom, happiness and getting what you want.
- Your collection of knowledge along with experience develops wisdom.
- The advantages of wisdom are increased common sense and intuition, as well as being more open to new ideas. You are more objective and independent in decision making. You get what you want faster, and you are happier, more loving and calm.
- The moment to take action is always now, as that is all there ever is. Any time you are ready, it will be now for you. Constantly postponing action leaves your dream life forever in the future.

EXERCISE: How to Discover Your Dreams

and Goals

1. Simply acknowledging to yourself that you are ready to discover your deepest dreams, goals and desires means you have the intention to know them. You will become open to discovering what really inspires you. These messages can arrive in numerous ways: you may have a sense inside you, you may see an advertisement you've never noticed before, you may meet someone with an interest that fascinates you, and so on.

2. Once you have the intention to discover your real dreams and interests, get quiet within yourself. You may sit, take a walk or spend some time on a quiet, relaxing hobby. The key is to be still within, and get lost in thought. Be truly present with your body by initially noticing the sensations in your body. Tell yourself this is an opportunity to know more about your deeper dreams, interests and aspects of life. This creates a purpose. Have a pen and paper handy and write down anything that pops into your head, including complaints. Later, reflect on these ideas and see if any create an urge in you to pursue them. Do this several times, and eventually you will have a good knowledge of what you want. Also capture anything that pops into your mind whenever you're daydreaming.

3. Ensure the dreams and interests that arise are yours and not someone else's. Ensure they are inspirational to you, and that they are not merely appealing to you because they may impress others. You need to own your dreams and be passionate about them to have the motivation to achieve them. We can be hard on ourselves when we don't achieve our goals, so be sure the goals you set are inspirational and worthy of focus.

4. Keep in mind that if you don't have your own dreams, you may well get caught up in following other people's dreams.

5. Later in the book, we'll discuss how to go about achieving goals.

Learning, discovering, creating and evolving starts with an idea or a dream and a willingness to participate in life.

EXERCISE: How to Start Developing Awareness, Truth and Wisdom

1. Start using any knowledge you have gained and include it as part of your daily life. Today is always a great day to begin.
2. Create an intention to notice your thoughts and feelings during situations.
a. Friends:
   Notice your topics of conversation with friends. What is the tone of the discussion? Do you talk about other people? How do you feel during the conversation, and how do you feel when you leave the conversation? Observe your opinions and beliefs about matters.
b. Other people:
   If you meet someone you like, ascertain what makes you like that person. If you meet someone who annoys you, establish what it is about them that annoys you, and try to learn something about yourself from that. If someone says something to you that upsets you, try to be objective, seeing it as feedback instead of having a knee-jerk reaction. Even if you recognize it for what it was after the knee-jerk reaction, it is still progress in developing awareness.
c. Daydreams:
   Observe your daydreams, for example while you are in the shower, while brushing your teeth, while driving or walking. What was the topic of the daydream? Did you have uplifting thoughts, or were you complaining to yourself about something?
d. Interests and accomplishments:
   Start to notice your special interests and accomplishments. Notice what holds your attention. Awareness of yourself enhances your ability to follow the path that's best for you.
e. Television and books:
   What television programs do you watch and what books do you read? Determine what they tell you about yourself and what you are thinking. What attracts you to them, and what is the reason for this?

f.   News:

When someone gives you bad news, what is your initial reaction? What about when someone else gets good news; what are your feelings? What are your comments about newspaper articles and the people featured in them? Do you sympathize or criticize? Every comment and feeling is a reflection of you, of which you must become aware.

3.   When making a decision, we only have opinions based on past experiences available to us. For changes and new adventures, you need to listen closely to your soul, so take notice of the different feelings in your body depending on which choice you make. Some may feel heavier, others lighter – you will know which one is the higher path from your feelings. These feelings provide you with greater awareness so you can act with integrity and harmony. You may still feel apprehensive prior to making a change in your life or trying something new. Feeling apprehensive is normal; it ensures you are alert and focused.

4.   Read other books that focus on developing awareness.

EXERCISE: Accessing Your Wisdom

1.   Slow down in your life and take moments for conscious reflection.

2.   When you have a decision to make, or someone wants an immediate answer from you, resist the temptation to reply instantly; instead, pause before answering. Choose the higher path for you when making a decision. Choose the decision that makes you feel lighter and liberated.

Section 2

You Are Responsible for Your Life

"Man blames fate for other accidents, but feels personally responsible when he makes a hole-in-one."

Unknown

*I*n addition to gaining knowledge and applying it, achieving happiness and what you want involves taking responsibility for the life you are living, healing any unwanted emotions and, of course, always loving yourself throughout the process. Human beings generally avoid admitting or taking responsibility, unless it is for something wonderful. The concept of being responsible for everything in your life is not new, and you've probably heard it before, but do you really understand what it means?

When completely understood, this knowledge has a dramatic effect on the way you involve yourself in the world.

The following chapters show you where and how to take responsibility in your life.

CHAPTER 3

Whatever You Think Is True

"Whether you believe you can do a thing or not, you are right."

Henry Ford
(Founder of Ford Motor Company,
1863–1947)

*Y*our thoughts can either create a prison for you or provide you with endless freedom. The thoughts you choose affect everything in your life, and are pivotal to your happiness, to getting what you want and to your health.[4]

You are the one who decides your thoughts.

In his book *The Hidden Messages in Water*, Masaru Emoto uses photographs of water crystals to demonstrate the effect of words on water. Mr Emoto found that positive expressions spoken to or written on a bottle of water created beautiful, well-formed crystals, while negative expressions barely formed any crystals, and the few that were created were malformed and fragmented. The photographs are astonishing. The average human body is 70% water, therefore every thought you have directly affects your body in this way. You can either create magic in your body, or a mangled mess. Your thoughts are this powerful.[8]

The Downsides of Survival Mode

Most of our thoughts are based on habitual emotions and instincts, which are linked to our past and to our DNA.[3,4] Therefore most people select thoughts unconsciously, impulsively, habitually. If their emotions are ones of lack, self-pity or jealousy, then that is the life experienced.

> *"If you do not change direction you may end up where you are heading."*
>
> Lao Tzu
> (Chinese Taoist philosopher and founder of Taoism, 600–531 BC)

If a person is unaware of what they are doing, their body acts alone, without wisdom and guidance, and their core purpose for living is simply survival.[3] People who are in survival mode usually blame others for their lives, judge others, feel sorry for themselves, are quick to anger, and live in fear. They also probably feel there isn't enough to go around, believe that others are luckier and overlook the blessings in their lives. Of course, much of this comes from their past and their DNA, as well as the culture of their surroundings. Living this way becomes such a habit that it creates a comfort zone, even if it is uncomfortable!

Needless to say, survival mode is somewhat limiting, and tends to dominate, regardless of whether the person wants change in their life or not. As we learnt earlier, change rings an alarm bell. It creates an unpredictable situation, a 'threat'. When something is unpredictable, there is no guarantee of survival, so the body resists change in an attempt to reduce risk.[3] Life becomes dull and uneventful, littered with disappointment. We don't know why at the time, but this causes us to become disgruntled with our life. This fuels the cycle of blaming others, anger and so on.

Where Your Thoughts Come From

Your thoughts come from a consciousness flowing through you. This consciousness is like a river of thought, ensuring that a continuous stream of unlimited information, images, ideas and concepts keeps running through your mind. This consciousness is everywhere, in all of us in every moment.[3]

You decide which thought potentials – uplifting or limiting – to choose from out of this flow of consciousness. Of course, for those who are unaware of their thoughts, the choices are unconscious and haphazard. These thoughts become your mind.

The Thoughts You Choose = Your Life

According to quantum physicists, the thoughts you choose end up becoming a physical substance or event.[1, 3] This is seen in the water crystal pictures mentioned earlier. Your God within doesn't judge your thoughts, but allows you free will to think and therefore create whatever you choose.[3]

The consciousness flowing through us contains thoughts at a range of frequencies. Lower frequency thoughts include fear, blame, victimization, disease and competition. Higher frequency thoughts consist of love, harmony, happiness, wisdom, infinite potential and so on. Science has demonstrated that there is more power in a higher frequency. The frequency at which you vibrate attracts corresponding thoughts to you, which in turn attract subatomic particles of a similar frequency.[3]

This is how ideal people, situations and things 'magically' appear in your life. This is often called coincidence, but a coincidence is not simply a matter of luck; it is a result of your thoughts. Your entire being vibrates at a certain frequency depending on your thoughts, therefore everything you think becomes what you have in your life, which is why other people have different things in their lives. You've heard people say, 'We're on the same wavelength.' Well, they're right, because we attract people and things with a similar wavelength. By attracting your life you create your life, which is the reality in which you live. It is a one-to-one correlation.

Every material item was originally a thought, which makes perfect sense when you realize that every item on Earth was initially imagined by someone, and then created into something physical. Your thoughts attract physical items into your life – you don't have to figure out how they got to you. This concept applies to something concrete, like a household item, as well as intangible things, like a new relationship.

3 Whatever You Think Is True

"Happiness and love are just a choice away."

Leo F. Buscaglia
(Author of inspirational books, 1924–1998)

New Knowledge is Your Launch Pad

The value in learning this is that the more you understand who you are, the bigger the platform you have from which to launch your dream life. Your mind advances to higher thoughts and your frequency rises as you add to your knowledge. Your options become greater, and you attract people and circumstances with a similar higher frequency. By creating goals, you attract particles that are resonating with your frequency, and you get what you want. Of course, the same happens if you choose lower frequency thoughts; you attract people, situations and things with a lower frequency. It's best not to hang out there.

More Scientific Proof of the Power of Your Thought

Enter neuroplasticity. First, some background: this is the name given to the brain's ability to change itself and find a new way to function, even if part of it is damaged. *Neuro* means nerve, and here it means the nerve cells that constitute the brain, spinal column and nervous system. *Plastic* means flexible, capable of being shaped, modified or influenced.

It was previously thought that certain parts of the brain exclusively governed certain activities of the body, and if that part of the brain was damaged, there was no hope, but scientists have since proven otherwise. For instance, stroke victims are now relearning how to use parts of their body in ways that were previously thought impossible.[6, 7]

It seems that even science struggles with change, because neuroplasticity was yet another discovery kept under wraps for fear of retribution. For hundreds of years, conventional neuroscience had believed that the brain was fixed, and they wanted it to stay that way. In many cases, the belief in a fixed brain was so great that not even solid scientific proof was sufficiently convincing to overcome it. Finally, however, they accepted the evidence that the brain can repair damage, grow

41

new neurons, move regions and change its circuitry – that it can be rewired.[6, 7]

The importance of neuroplasticity for our purposes is that scientists have found that in many cases it is focused *thought* that harnesses the brain's neuroplastic ability to provide amazing health solutions.

In particular, experiments have proved that many people with mental disorders such as obsessive compulsive disorder and depression can be remedied through focused thought. Even for those without a disorder, neuroplasticity is showing that we can train our mind for greater happiness and compassion, just as we can learn a musical instrument, learn to swim or learn to play golf.[6, 7]

> *"The message I take from my own work is that I have a choice in how I react, that who I am depends on the choices I make, and that who I am is therefore my responsibility."*
> Dr. Richard J Davidson
> (Research professor of psychology and psychiatry and director of the W.M. Keck Laboratory for Functional Brain Imaging and Behavior and the Laboratory for Affective Neuroscience, University of Wisconsin-Madison.
> *Source:* Train Your Mind, Change Your Brain by Sharon Begley)

And if that's not enough good news, studies in neuroplasticity have confirmed that meditation and creative visualization are powerful tools in assisting the brain to renew itself. These ideas have been around a long time, but for the most part we've simply had to 'believe' they work. Now, however, we have scientific proof. For example, experiments show that if people visualize themselves doing physical exercise, there are detectable and measurable changes in the motor neurons of the brain. Subsequent studies proved that these people actually became physically stronger.[6, 7]

Another reason for continually adding to your knowledge is that it keeps you tuned in to discovering amazing breakthroughs such as neuroplasticity, which buoy us and fill us with inspiration.

Determination and focus are essential if you are to create these changes in your life, but you now know you have the choice to change your life. Intention to change takes you half way there. Change your thoughts, and change your life.

Anything You Want is Already There for You

Whatever you want for your future already exists as a potential on the quantum field. There are infinite potentials of anything you want, all happening at the same time. You decide what to focus on, and therefore what you will have. If you decide to focus on wealth or health, then that is what you will get. If you focus on poverty or illness, then that is what you will get. *You choose*. The quantum field is your universe.[3]

Hypnosis uniquely demonstrates the potentials of the brain. Watching television one evening, my family saw a hypnotist working with a group of young adults. Most people find hypnosis fascinating, and we weren't any different. The hypnotist set up a classroom scene in the minds of the group whereby they were told they were nine-year-old children who misbehaved whenever he was out of the room. They were also told to lie about their behavior when he returned. He left the room and, as planned, they caused all sorts of trouble. That was hilarious enough, but when the hypnotist returned, he set it up that their tongues would feel like they were on fire if they lied. As expected, each person lied, and when they did so, they then struggled with the sensation of a burning tongue. As soon as he snapped them back to reality, their tongues felt normal.

The brain believes what it is told. This is the power of the brain, and you can produce this magic in your life even without hypnosis.

The Easiest Way to Break Free From Your Captivity

Flip the switch and become aware of your thoughts; purposefully choose your thoughts, according to what you want. Once the light is on, you can't turn it off. The darkness is gone, and you know how the universe functions. Conscious, intentional thinking eventually becomes a habit. When you choose thoughts intentionally, you are tapping into your deep inner knowing which comes from your soul. Selecting thoughts of potential and dreaming new possibilities is fun, and surely preferable to feeling lost, angry, without purpose, fearful, confused, scared or sad.

> *"Man's mind, once stretched by a new idea, never regains its original dimensions."*
>
> Oliver Wendell Holmes, Jr.
> (American judge and jurist, who was called 'The Great Dissenter', for he often disagreed with the conservative majority, 1841–1935)

Break free from captivity and choose awareness in every moment – be accountable for your thoughts. Change one thought at a time. Be deliberately present, because in every moment you are creating a thought, and therefore your life, and everything you want.

Summary of

"Whatever You Think Is True"

- Thoughts either create a prison for you or provide your freedom.
- Your thoughts affect everything in your life.
- The consciousness flowing through us is a river of thought, from which we choose our potentials or limitations.
- Our thoughts create our reality through the quantum field. Everything we want is available to us. We are free to create whatever we choose.
- Every material item on Earth was originally a thought.
- Your thoughts have a specific frequency, which draw objects, people and situations with a similar frequency to you.
- The higher your thoughts the higher the frequency of your vibration. As you raise your frequency, you attract people and situations to match that frequency, and magically or coincidentally, they start to appear in your life. Some of these people may have always been around, but you never noticed each other before.
- Become aware of your thoughts and consciously choose them.

♦ You are creating your life in every moment.

EXERCISE: How to Consciously Choose Thoughts

Stay aware of your thoughts and if unhelpful, unwanted thoughts come up then you can do one or both of the following:

a) Say, 'No' to the thought and replace it with a carefully chosen powerful thought (have some ready). Unwanted thoughts come from the past, from the old program of habitual limited attitudes and beliefs. They are on an addictive cycle and they keep you in your past. By saying, 'No', you are taking control, breaking the cycle, reprogramming your brain and over time your powerful thoughts will dominate.

b) Focus on being *present* with what you are doing, in this moment. Thoughts from your past cannot function in the present. So when you consciously move to the 'now', they disappear.

1. Choose an issue on which you would like to work.
2. Start with gratitude for everything your current circumstance has provided for you, including the wisdom and the motivation to change.
3. Spend a week catching your thoughts on the subject. Do whatever it takes; keep a small notebook on you for this purpose. Divide the page into two columns.
4. In one column, write down how you currently express yourself.
5. Then, in the other column, re-write the sentence using positive sentences commencing with 'I am…', 'I have…', or 'I choose….'

Limiting Thought	The New You
I can't afford that	I have everything I want and need. I have abundant wealth. I choose to buy that later.

I hate being fat	I love my body the way it is. My body is special. I'm gorgeous. I love what I see in me.
I can't lose weight	The food I eat maintains my ideal weight. My body is the ideal weight for me. I easily maintain the ideal weight for me.
Nobody cares	I love myself and I enjoy great relationships with others. I am surrounded and embraced by love. I find others to be caring and loving.
I'm no good	I am a special, unique and powerful person. I can achieve anything I choose. I am a remarkable and wonderful person.

Play with words that bring about a shift within you. Have fun with them. State it as if you have this thing already, because somewhere on the quantum field you actually do have it, and now you want to use your thought to focus there, and bring it in. Someone with an issue with their weight may do nothing about their eating, yet change their life significantly when they change their attitude. Notice the difference in your attitude when you choose a higher potential, a greater thought.

6. For each new statement, imagine an image or a symbol that represents the new you.[4] It can be anything at all. Sit quietly, and it will quickly appear to you. Draw the symbol on a card, using colours if you wish. Your brain understands what it represents. Place it beside your bed, and focus on it before going to sleep and as often as you can each day.

CHAPTER 4

You Are Creating
Your Life Right Now

"Responsibility is the price of greatness."

Winston Churchill

(U.K. Prime Minister 1940–1945, 1951–1955, noted for his speeches, 1874–1965)

*Y*ou have created your life, every detail of it, and there's no escaping this.[3] Being responsible for your life means you cannot blame anyone else for your life. This is a powerful and vitally important message.

Once you embrace being responsible for your life and start taking responsibility, you have immediate empowerment and freedom to create what you want in your life. This is because responsibility grants you the power to actively create your brilliant life.

"Our lives are a sum total of the choices we have made."

Wayne Dyer

(American motivational speaker and author of self-help books, b. 1940)

You Are Choosing Your Life In Every Moment

This responsibility means that you, and only you, have created the current state of your health, the people in your

47

life, your possessions, your financial situation, your job, your work colleagues, where you live and your feelings. Pause for a moment and contemplate these aspects of your life. You've chosen all of them, and all of your experiences. This continues in every moment your heart beats – you continue creating your life. In fact, you're also creating your heartbeat in every moment; you are doing it all.

This can be motivating to some and discouraging to others. It may be overwhelming to think that you created everything that is dissatisfying in your life, but wait…there's brilliance in this. If you've been creating your life so far without realizing it, it follows that it is *you* who has the *power* to change everything by *intentionally* creating a different life. From today, if you embrace these ideas, your whole life jumps to a higher, more exciting one of your choosing. Decide purposefully to choose abundance, compassion and love for yourself and others, instead of scarcity, anger and fear. Pick which frequencies you would like to attract. It's free, and it's easy, so go for it!

It's Easy to Accept Responsibility When You're Having Fun

Many people I've spoken to have nodded convincingly, appearing to understand this message. Initially, they picture this as a great concept, however subsequent adversity quickly returns them to their old patterns, and they soon discard our conversation and their responsibility. It certainly requires mental effort to take responsibility for our lives, to shove blame aside and to be truly honest with ourselves. In the moment, blaming someone can seem the most obvious and easy solution. We pretend it has nothing to do with us, and we immerse ourselves in self-pity.

That feels good momentarily, but it means we're avoiding responsibility, and it shuts down our power.

Facing Responsibility is The Key to Your Power

It's your decision as to which path you choose. Do you want others to decide and control your life, or do you want to do it?

To be completely sure you understand this concept of responsibility, I've included some examples for you to contemplate. In every example, the person creates the issue, each of which has a message. If you have anything like any one of these issues in your life, try to be objective about the incident, and use the exercises below to change your life.

> *"It's easy to dodge our responsibility, but we cannot dodge the consequences of dodging our responsibility."*
>
> Josiah Charles Stamp
> (Director of the Bank of England in the 1920s and reputed to be Great Britain's second-richest man, 1880 – 1941)

Examples of Taking Responsibility

1. When it comes to car accidents, people usually say they had nothing to do with what happened; it was the other person's fault. In the eyes of the law, this may be so, but if we are involved, we created the situation. There is no fault or blame, merely the question as to why our car was involved. It's not bad or good luck; somehow, we attracted that person to collide with us. The event requires contemplation.

2. Getting a cold or flu is usually seen as unfortunate, but people can only get colds if they are open to receiving them. In fact, it is likely they have been feeling overwhelmed, confused, depressed or have the attitude that they 'always catch colds' and so on. Each person can have a different reason for getting sick.

3. When someone breaks an arm, or suffers some similar injury, they're seen as unlucky. Being hurt usually brings added love and attention into our lives. Somehow there is an advantage, and it resonates with the pattern of their thoughts.

4. When a sales person is rude, the tendency is to blame the sales person, although when anyone is rude to us, we attract their behavior. In these situations, we need to look at our self-respect, self-worth, and so on. Something about our thoughts attracts people to behave like that.

5. A manager who is nasty or annoying to us may also be difficult for others to deal with, but our thoughts and attitude can turn this manager into someone who treats us well. We must be willing to be flexible in our attitude and

communication. Even if people speak unfavourably about this manager, you can choose to be the person who gets along with them. You could help everyone else to learn to get along with them. If you can get along with anyone, you are an asset in any organization. This can also be applied to other areas of our lives. A harmonious path can always be achieved.

6. Divorce or separation usually involves blaming the partner, but we must consider that the thoughts of both partners allowed or encouraged the situation. The only way through is to focus on our contribution to the partnership, and the fact that we participated in its breakdown – not by blaming ourselves, but by accepting the responsibility that we have the power to, and *do*, create our own situations.

7. People who take advantage of us have been allowed to do so. We cannot expect others to know how to treat us appropriately. We teach others how to treat us. They will only treat us appropriately if we feel worthwhile.

8. A bad childhood is often blamed on others. This can be a sensitive subject, as many people endured a tragic childhood, but if we are waiting or hoping for someone to acknowledge our heartache, we could wait a lifetime. Instead, if we can somehow empower ourselves, we benefit far more than we do through self-pity or by waiting for an acknowledgement that may never come. Many people who have achieved amazing success attribute it to the moulding they had through adversity as a child. Once we become an adult, it is to our advantage to move on from blame and use the wisdom learnt from our childhood. Self-pity causes people to live in their past, but this is detrimental in the long-term as they are missing out on the magical life they could have today. There is more about this in chapter 32 on *Forgiveness*.

If you don't feel ready to take responsibility, I suggest that you merely consider this concept as a possibility. There is no need to absolutely accept this, just as there is no reason to accept anything anyone tells you. I merely ask you to keep an open mind.

It may be uncomfortable recognizing that these examples relate to you, but it is helpful for your growth if any such recognition was triggered. Even if you want to avoid taking responsibility for the car accident, for the nasty manager, and so on, remember that avoiding responsibility means giving away your power – your key to your future.

This is not about revenge or karma: behavior is never good or bad. The quantum field simply attracts to you whatever you put out. It is advantageous to develop an understanding that there is no right or wrong and no good or bad. Everything that happens expands your wisdom. Every experience happens for that reason. The less you differentiate between good and bad, the more you will accept the polarities of life on Earth and get what you want.[3]

Building Pathways in Your Brain

Acting 'as if', or pretending, is a wonderful way to get started in choosing your greater life. Decide what you would like to become, and start acting 'as if' that is who you are. As much as you can, align your thoughts each day with this dream. Use affirmations such as, 'I am… (*insert whatever you want*).'

When your brain sees those words, neurons fire and a new pathway instantly starts forming in your brain. As you focus less and less on the old way, those pathways in your brain diminish, until eventually they are no more. Imagine a track formed by people walking through bush land. When no one walks there any more, the grass starts growing over the track until one day the track is gone. By choosing new thoughts, you've created a new pathway that's alive and well in your brain, and those thoughts contain your magnificent life. Continually focus on going there, and over time that pathway in your brain collects even more neurons and becomes stronger. Every time you choose higher thoughts, it becomes easier to hold onto them.

Every Thought is a Choice You Are Making – Make it Count

It is empowering to know that you have choice in a matter, and that you can change your mind at any time. Use the exercises below to practice exploring your own examples of difficult situations where you could take responsibility. Once you become aware of them, you can deliberately take the higher path.

Keep in mind all those things you love about your life – remember, you created them, too.

Taking responsibility is all about attitude – when you're in charge of your thoughts, you'll get what you want. Make every thought count, and make every day great.

Summary of

"You Are Creating Your Life Right Now"

- You have created every detail of your life.
- Once you start taking responsibility for your life, you have immediate empowerment and freedom to create the life you would rather have.
- Whatever you think and focus on most of the time will be the life you are experiencing now.
- People are usually happy to consider that they are responsible for their lives, until their next adversity.
- It is an effort to take responsibility, and it is our choice whether we do so or not. The alternative is to forever have others decide for us and control our lives.
- If this is a challenging concept for you, then merely keep an open mind to the possibilities of this idea.
- Pretending, or acting 'as if' you already have a wonderful life, is an ideal way to get started.
- Choose to make every day great.

EXERCISE: How to Take Responsibility

for Your Life

Your Current Life:
1. Consider your life – the aspects you are proud of and those you are not. Include relationships, health, finances, your home, current beliefs, attitudes, your friends and 'enemies', your children and their behavior, and so on.

2. Make a list of each: one column for those aspects you like and one for those you don't.
3. Ponder each list and recognize that you created everything in those lists. This action alone takes you a long way to realizing they weren't due to good luck, bad luck or because of other people. It was all you.
4. Assess whether you are able to acknowledge this, and the current challenges in your life.
5. It is all right if you can't acknowledge it yet. By asking yourself the question, you have already started to open your mind to new potentials.
6. Recognize that this exercise is not to apportion blame. Each list contains things that made you who you are today, and each is as valuable as the other. Neither is right or wrong – only your opinion tells you that.
7. The purpose of this exercise is to highlight the fact that your inner power created all of that, so imagine if you became aware of your thoughts and consciously focused on an extraordinary life.

Outside Influences on Your Life:

When you decide to take responsibility for your life, the media is a great place to start. We are fed a lot of information via the media, most of which has nothing to do with us and is unhelpful and unnecessary. Choose to be responsible for which movies you choose, what you are exposed to on TV and what you read in books, newspapers and magazines. The news on TV is not an ideal path to higher thoughts. Most topics are sad, violent and hopeless. You now know that whatever your focus, you get it back. Also, when we are watching passively, being fed stories one after the other, unaware of what is coming next, we are a captive audience, and we're not just hearing it; we're also receiving a powerful visual message. Life is serious enough without watching other people's misery. We need to make it as easy as possible for us to be happy. What you expose yourself to affects your mood and how you think. If you do choose to watch the news on TV, do so with objectivity and an enquiring mind.

Reading the newspaper or a news website on the Internet is an alternative; this way, you are not being fed the information without choice. Instead, you can choose which articles to read, and the violent or disheartening stories aren't as graphic.

Most importantly, choose what you watch before bedtime. Most entertainment on TV is about murder, robbery, court cases and hospital dramas. Sometimes it is someone else's real-life drama, their devastation and agony…just what you need, right? If you go to sleep with thoughts of murder, fear, apathy or sadness, your dreams reflect that. Rather, watch something inspiring, or a comedy. Find laughter wherever you can. Laughter is cleansing and energizing. It enables you to let go of the world, and your frequency is lifted higher. Then, before going to sleep, try to read a book that fills you with possibility. Your dreams will then be of possibility and wonder. We can choose to surround ourselves with the most nourishing environment possible.

Avoid the herd mentality; you should always consciously choose what is best for you.

CHAPTER 5

Challenges are Powerful Opportunities for You

"Opportunities to find deeper powers within ourselves come when life seems most challenging."

Joseph Campbell

(American author, philosopher and teacher, 1904–1987)

Challenges need to be viewed with a new perception. Challenges aren't 'bad luck' – they are an opportunity to discover something wonderful! Your thoughts create your life, therefore they also create challenges in your life.[4] When you take responsibility for creating your challenges, you take back your power. Your attitude toward handling challenges will either take you toward fulfilling your purposes on Earth, or they will take you toward more frustration.

Challenges as an Asset

You usually create your challenges when you are not on your ideal path, or have lost track of your thoughts and actions. If you're not on your ideal path, it's unlikely you will be getting what you want. Note: there is another form of challenge that appears when we have consciously made major changes in our lives. Initially, those changes can seem to create more challenges. There will be more on this later. Here, however, we are talking about situations that appear when we are still haphazard and unaware in our thinking.

While it is not always easy to see it that way, challenges are feedback as to how and where you need to grow and change your attitude. Most people call them 'problems', but they can provide amazing discoveries and new experiences to enable you to master your body and catapult you to a different destiny. When challenges cause you to pause and ponder what this is all about, you are becoming ready to engage them for growth. This is a great sign, because challenges suddenly become a remarkable asset.

Adversity Will Get Your Attention

If you are encountering constant challenges, then it is vital that you assess your life. It's usually a sign of ignoring too many minor challenges, which are sometimes called 'taps' on the shoulder. Constant challenges will hopefully get your attention.

> *"Some people change their ways when they see the light,*
> *others when they feel the heat."*
>
> Caroline Schroeder

Challenges highlight what really matters to you in life. There's nothing like adversity to quickly get your attention. It is that initial rotten feeling or awful experience that motivates you to change and grow. Given the appropriate level of discomfort, you will take a closer look at your life, otherwise you would just carry on the way you were. Some people have to hit rock bottom before 'getting the message'. Adversity should be enough to grab your attention so you can immediately reflect on why this happened, and how you can avoid it in the future. Challenges can be an excellent way of creating wisdom, because you are forced into taking action in a situation, and your understanding about yourself and life grows as you overcome each challenge.

> *"We know the true worth of a thing when we have lost it."*
>
> French Proverb

A new perspective arrives with challenges.

When Trisha broke her leg, it changed her life, but it also changed her husband's life radically. Initially, he stayed home as her full-time carer, and rapidly went from being someone who grumbled about his job to someone who couldn't wait to get back to work. He started seeing his regular life as something worth appreciating. We'll discuss this again later in Chapter 16 on *Gratitude*.

Challenges could be in any area of your life – family, career, health, relationships, mental health, and so on. Anything you complain about is a potential challenge, and a wonderful opportunity for change and a different attitude. Eventually, when you are ready, you will find that you are motivated to shed some light on the meaning of a challenge. As with discovering your interests and goals, reflection about a challenge gives you answers about what you should be doing instead.

"Learn to get in touch with the silence within yourself and know that everything in life has purpose. There are no mistakes, no coincidences, all events are blessings given to us to learn from."

Elisabeth Kubler-Ross
(Swiss-American psychiatrist and author, 1926–2004)

Reduce the Heat by Using Your Feedback

You will continue to be challenged until you detect the meaning of the challenges, or until you indicate to yourself that you are ready to learn and change. It won't all happen at once, but if you are objective and aware, you will notice a pattern in challenges. For example, if you were working on forgiveness issues, you would consistently be faced with situations over a period of time where forgiveness was required. The first step would be to surrender to the challenges, go within and conclude that forgiveness is the issue. The second step would be to learn to forgive. Often, it is this second step that is most difficult, and people often duck and dive to avoid it, but until it is accomplished, the challenges continue.

Once accomplished, that type of situation is no longer encountered. The reason is that your thoughts and attitude have changed. On top of that, you find that you have also grown in other areas of your life. There is a ripple effect – everything is related. You receive wonderful rewards, as if the world is smiling on you. ☺

Never Put Up With Something That Makes You Unhappy

Never give up on finding an ideal answer to a challenge. It may not seem like it, but the knowledge you gain along the way and the changes you implement release you into freedom, and what you want gets closer. Even if you're confused as to what the challenge means, your intention to know starts the changes immediately, and your insight develops. Seek further knowledge until you understand.

"There is always a way – if you're committed."
Anthony Robbins
(American self-help writer, b. 1960)

If you have a sincere commitment to finding a solution, your breakthrough will be imminent. If you are half-hearted, you'll have no focus, your thoughts will be scattered and there will be confusion as to exactly what it is you want.

Become centered and clear about your desire. Keep going until you find a solution. You will feel uplifted as soon as you take action. Never put up with something that makes you unhappy. Each challenge is encouraging you to change, to discover new aspects about your life or to have new experiences. These are important to your growth and happiness. Sometimes, the best parts of your life are discovered via adversity. Adversity is very often what places people on their path.

Growing Through Joy

Growing through challenges is tough work unless we change our attitude toward them. Instead of refusing to face challenges, decide to face them with the freedom of an open mind and confidence. When you become more alert and optimistic in your life and recognize a challenge for what it is, you get to spring over that rotten feeling or awful experience into a bright world of possibility.

As you resist the survival instincts of the body and listen to and follow the higher path of your soul's whispers, your growth is easier and you are open to create your ideal destiny. You enjoy greater flow in your life.

By paying attention, you become tuned in to the first sign of a challenge. You act at the prompt of a small challenge, you even become proactive and act before the challenge arrives, and you see the potential by viewing it from a greater perspective. You actively seek opportunities to grow, and you begin to recognize that you can handle anything that comes your way.

A situation is neither good nor bad.[3] Most situations can be viewed in several ways. There is always a higher perspective, so it is up to you as to how you determine a situation. Just as your body gets stronger and fitter with continual physical exercise, so too will you find choosing the greater viewpoint easier with practice, until in the end it becomes habitual.

Just When You Thought You Had It All Worked Out

Even when you have consciously chosen to follow a path to your greatest life, challenges may still be encountered. Ideally we are always evolving and challenges provide appropriate circumstances for rapid change and growth. Again, they are not a 'bad' thing, they are an opportunity. Maintain a carefree, light heart and it may not even end up being a challenge at all. Often, we can't imagine how a situation will unfold, and this lack of knowing can be concerning. If you find yourself facing a challenge, tell yourself, 'This is a great opportunity for something wonderful, and I'm keeping an open mind.' Your body will feel greatly reassured.

Your Very Own Special Challenges

Everyone's path is different, and so are their challenges. What is challenging to one person is a mild stumble, or perhaps nothing, to the next person. Some people have multiple challenges happening at once, while others only have minor inconveniences. It depends on your attitude, and what you are attracting into your life. Focus only on your life, and what is happening in it. Avoid analyzing other people's lives.

Compassion

As you overcome challenges, you are more likely to empathize with others when they struggle, and you are more willing to accept people, no matter what their behavior.

Your Fork in the Road

Once you understand that challenges are a path to a greater life, you'll face them with openness, because you have discovered their power. You have the knowledge to overcome them, and you know they carry you to wonderful places. You'll grow through joy.

Challenges are an ideal catalyst to bring your dream life towards you.

Summary of
"Challenges Are Powerful
Opportunities for You"

+ Challenges occur if the reasons you came to Earth are not being fulfilled, if you're not evolving or if your current choices aren't helpful.
+ Challenges illustrate how you are thinking, because your thoughts create your challenges.
+ You usually create your challenges when your course in life is off beam or you are living each day without conscious thought. If you're not on your ideal path, it's unlikely you will be getting what you want.
+ Challenges reveal what really matters in life.
+ Challenges provide perspective.
+ Challenges are opportunities for discovery, and opportunities to change your destiny.
+ Contemplate your challenges to find out what you could be thinking and doing instead.
+ Overcoming challenges help us to better understand ourselves and accept others.
+ A certain challenge to one person may be nothing to the next.

- Never give up on finding an answer to a challenge. The challenges will continue or keep reappearing until you change.
- Become proactive at the first sign of a challenge.
- Try facing challenges with anticipation and recognize the value they can provide.
- Situations are neither good nor bad. It depends on your perception.
- A challenge can be a catalyst to spur you on to your dream life.

EXERCISE: How to Handle Challenges

1. As soon as you become aware of the situation as a challenge, move to a place of stillness and say to yourself something like, 'I would like to know what to do; I am ready to listen', or 'What part of me do I need to develop to get past this challenge?' You are creating an intention to tap into your soul's wisdom. Don't expect logic to play a part: you are allowing yourself to go *beyond* your senses. Allow your attention to remain on the question. If necessary, keep repeating it, so that you remain focused and are sufficiently aware to pick up the answer. Throughout the day, try to be alert for any insights.

2. You may choose to imagine yourself next to you, and engage in a conversation with yourself. Ask yourself questions about the meaning of the challenge, and what you could be doing instead. Ask yourself how you can grow. Tell yourself you are ready to change. Be still, and listen for the reply.

3. Practice handling challenges as merely feedback, and another step in your progress. Recognize that you are in the middle of a teaching. Tackle challenges as you would any other task. Let your emotions flow without analyzing or labelling them. They aren't good or bad – just let them be. *Pretending* to remain neutral also works.

4. Even if you can't work out what you need to change, merely indicating to yourself that you are ready to listen will bring

about changes. It may not be a conscious understanding for you, and you may muddle your way through, but by listening to the whispers of your soul (your conscience) and using intention and determination, you will begin to head in the ideal direction for you, one day at a time.

5. Once you have some ideas, create some inspirational affirmations, so as to focus your thoughts on getting what you want. They are covered in more detail at the end of this book in Section 6 *The Gift of Every New Day*. Write them on cards and place them around the house and at work.

6. Changes will start to happen, even if you are unaware of them. Not that you become nonchalant, just know that your determination is integral to creating changes, which may be beyond your ability to comprehend.

7. If unwanted thoughts keep surfacing, follow the instructions in the exercise 'How to Consciously Choose Thoughts' in Chapter 3 *Whatever You Think Is True*.

8. Release any emotions you feel during a challenge, even if you haven't worked out their meaning. Say, 'I accept that there is a message in this for me.' The intention to move on is what is significant. Use the *Release Emotion Technique* (see Appendix A).

9. During challenges, you will cope better by staying in the present moment, so if you find yourself drifting to the past or the future, keep placing yourself in the present again and again. Try to focus on being grateful for your life and on enjoying what you do in each moment. If you are in the past, you re-experience old emotions and block your growth. If you are in the future, you may inadvertently create fear about what might happen. Being in the present keeps you happy, and it is in the *now* that you have the greatest ability to create powerful, lasting change.

CHAPTER 6

Everyone Is Your Teacher – Everyone Is Your 'Mirror'

"Friends are the mirror reflecting the truth of who we are."

The way people treat you is a direct reflection of what you think about yourself. We all enjoy happy interactions with others, but we must already have that cheerful approach to life in order to experience it in others. By taking responsibility for your life and being aware of your thoughts, you rise to a higher frequency, and you see only the best in other people.

Is That Really Me?

Until you rise above your own view of the world, you can only see your own limited reality, where everyone is *you*. You only resonate with your own frequency. If you are filled with unhappiness, you will attract unhappiness from others, and if you are happy, you will only see happiness in others. When we experience an unwanted attitude in someone, we must look at ourselves. You're not seeing them; you're seeing you. It's all about you. Agreed, it's a little weird, and often not obvious, but try it and you'll see; everyone is a mirror of you – they are your reflection.[3]

"Everything that irritates us about others can lead us to an understanding of ourselves."

Carl Gustav Jung
(Swiss psychiatrist and psychologist, 1875–1961)

People Behave According to What You Think

I was chatting to Jim, a flight attendant, who said that working with the public is challenging. He said that many passengers display extremely rude behavior, and vent their frustration on flight attendants. This can seem like a hopeless situation for anyone working with people on a mass scale, so let's assess it.

Firstly, life owes you nothing, and while you have every right to have people respect you, you *create* respect, just like everything else in your life. Secondly, if you can recognize unhappiness when you see it, you'll understand why someone is being rude. Thirdly, after several incidents with rude people, you may develop a fear about what people are likely to do next. We begin to protect ourselves by preparing for the next cold encounter, and guess what we get; more frosty people. Someone will only be rude to you if something about you attracts it. Never accept rudeness as a part of your life. If you face this every day as part of your job, do whatever it takes to look at yourself and change it.

Make it a goal to discover what changes you can make to yourself that will invite warmth and respect from people. Use this opportunity to grow.

Contemplate your thoughts and your attitudes. It may be anything, such as being disillusioned with humanity, lacking trust, hating your job, being apathetic, lacking self-respect, expecting grumpy people, being scared that people are out to hurt you, feeling powerless, and so on. You will only know by asking yourself.

"Maxim for life: You get treated in life the way you teach people to treat you."

Wayne Dyer
(American motivational speaker and author of self-help books, b. 1940)

The situation involving Jim described above can and does occur in many jobs. As you make changes within, you will notice a marked increase in the number of warm, friendly people you meet. They will be attracted to you, and you will be treated the way you want to be treated. If you experience disrespect, especially as you start out, stay empowered and intensify your efforts to understand yourself. Know that you have the answer, and that if you really want it, you will find it. Never give up.

You may even believe that you are sending out a message of welcome and expecting one in return, but your feedback says there is a bigger part of you that isn't doing this. Even if you can't identify the specific issue for you, brighten your thoughts to ones of freedom, such as, 'I have the power to attract friendly people', 'I only attract cheerful customers', or 'I have plenty of laughs with my customers today.' This may sound too simple, but it absolutely works. The only obstacle will be any doubts you have. As with all affirmations, make these thoughts a vibrant, inspirational part of your life. Place them on cards around your home and in your car to remind you of your goal. Buy into this strategy as much as you can; don't just 'wait and see' how it goes. Expect changes; pretend that it's already working. Even if the situation worsens, it indicates that change is happening. Keep going until you get what you want.

If you'd like a friendly exchange with every customer, then make that your goal. It may sound like a formidable task, but is it really? Your limits are whatever you think they are. Go for gold instead of limiting yourself. If your doubt is too great, feel free to lower the bar to something you consider achievable. You have the potential to achieve anything, and you will chalk up plenty of valuable wisdom along the way.

Of course, all this depends on how motivated you are to create change. A genuine intention will get you at least half way there.

Catching Your Reflection

"The quality of your life is the quality of your relationships."
Anthony Robbins
(American self-help writer, b. 1960)

It isn't necessarily easy to catch yourself in others' reflections, or to stop immediately and realize that it's you in the reflection. This is something that unfolds, but once you know why it happens, you are able to elect to work with yourself to do something about it. If you don't do anything about it, you're choosing not to, which is fine. Perhaps you'll do it next time.

It can be tough, but it is essential to be lovingly honest with yourself. Hiding issues or ignoring them is no solution. As with challenges, the situations keep coming up until they are dealt with appropriately. If you have found something about yourself that needs resolving, then taking action to find out how to resolve it puts you firmly on your path.

Let Go of Others and Simply Focus On You

Everyone becomes your teacher, and so to create your dream life, you *only* have to focus on your own thoughts and change yourself. Life is simplified.

To become even greater, release the need for others to be friendly or to approve of you. It's only *our* opinion of ourselves that matters. You empower yourself tremendously by letting go and being unconcerned about how others behave or think. Every time you empower yourself, you get more of what you want. This is because you no longer need someone else to be nice to you in order to be happy. It really doesn't matter how others behave or what they think of you. You decide your life, your happiness and whether you get what you want.

One Fine Day Your Reflection Reveals Your Harmony

As you evolve, you'll discover an absence of annoying traits in other people. When you get to this satisfying stage, people are likely to express only help, courtesy and friendliness toward you.

Notice and acknowledge helpful behaviour, encourage and reward it. Adults love this as much as children. As usual, you also gain an advantage by doing this. Making the effort to say something or write a thank you note means you continue to attract behaviour you want from others and they benefit from being appreciated. Everyone wins. (As always however, only do these if you *want* to, not because you have to.)

You Free Yourself When You Stop Waiting For Others to Behave

Your thoughts affect both you and the world around you. Trust yourself to take care of your thoughts, actions and, importantly, your reactions. Taking responsibility to create your life is far more satisfying than waiting for others to behave themselves so you can have a good time. Instead, punch the air and choose whether you have a good time or not. You have the power to shift your world. You are free…you are liberated…you fly higher.

Summary of

"Everyone Is Your Teacher – Everyone Is Your 'Mirror'"

♦   The way people treat you is a direct reflection of what you think about yourself.

♦   Things you dislike about others are things you dislike about yourself.

♦   Things that annoy you about others are things you do that annoy others.

♦   Everyone is a mirror of you.

♦   Have the courage to be honest with yourself when you aren't impressed with someone's behavior, remembering to love yourself along the way.

♦   Other people help us see who we really are and what we think of ourselves. This information helps us to change and build a greater life for ourselves.

♦   Release the need for others to be friendly and approve of you. Empower yourself by only relying on your own opinion. The opinion of others doesn't matter.

♦   As you evolve, you'll discover an absence of annoying traits in other people, who will show you only helpfulness and friendliness.

♦   Acknowledge and encourage helpful behavior, both from adults and children. This helps you to focus on the aspects you want in your life.

♦ Taking responsibility for your own life means you don't rely on others' behavior in order to enjoy yourself.

EXERCISE: How to See Your Own Reflection

1. Catch yourself noticing faults in others. Contemplate how that 'fault' relates to you – it is in your life somewhere. Ask yourself tough questions, like what it is about them that you can't completely accept, what made you feel the need to judge, and what was important about choosing a side. What did you gain from that? Note: it is preferable to use 'what' and 'how' questions and avoid 'why' questions so as to open up the brain for greater answers.

2. Catch yourself commenting on newspaper articles or current affairs. You'll notice your own beliefs and attitudes; you're discovering who you are.

3. Ask someone to gently indicate when you are criticizing others. This is not an opportunity for them to criticize you. Prepare yourself to accept this information graciously, as this is valuable for your growth. By helping you out, those whom you love also start to notice their own thoughts.

4. Observe when people complain about others, so that you can learn to be aware and present enough to recognize what people talk about. By doing this, you become proficient in preventing careless ideas from inadvertently entering your consciousness. Because you have an intention to notice other people's behavior, you will naturally become attuned to your own thoughts. As you become more aware of your thoughts and thereby avoid criticizing others, you will find that people around you complain less. This is because you no longer resonate with that behavior.

CHAPTER 7

Effectively Communicating With Others

"I know what I have given you. I do not know what you have received."

Antonio Porchia
(Italian poet, 1886–1968)

*W*hen you communicate with others, it is *up to you* to accurately deliver the information. The more precise your communication, the more you get what you want. Ideally, the responsibility you take with your life includes effective communication. Many misunderstandings or issues between people are due to ineffective communication.

My Reality Is Not Your Reality

It is important to understand that each of us lives in a different reality when it comes to our opinions, judgments, feelings, abundance, and so on. It is an illusion that we live in the same reality. This may sound crazy, as most people assume that everyone views the world the same way they do, and it does seem the same…from the point of view of our own reality. However, we filter each moment in our lives through our different DNA, culture, childhood, past lives and emotions.

We each react differently to the same event because of these different filters. We always focus on the part of the event that most resonates in our lives, either through pain or happiness. One person may hardly notice an event if it has no meaning, while for another person it could be fabulous, life changing, threatening, sad, and so on. Yet no one is right and no one is wrong. This is also the reason the 'truth' can be so different for each person.

Most people cannot claim to be completely objective in any situation. It is part of your journey to improve your objectivity, because the more open-minded you can be, the higher your thought frequency. Consequently, you will live a greater life. From this higher vantage point, you can understand other people's behavior. You'll be less likely to judge their choices if you realize that they may well consider your choices irrational, too. This makes more sense once you learn why you are on Earth, and that we each have different aspects of ourselves to master.

This truly is our own little world.

The Elegance of *Your* Delivery

You cannot blame others for their inability to understand your words. If someone doesn't understand you or ignores you, it is your responsibility, not theirs. Most people joke about or criticize other people's inability to understand them. We hear people say, 'I told her but she just didn't get it', or 'He just doesn't listen.' They don't realize that they are criticizing their own inability to get their point across accurately. You are responsible for finding a harmonious way to communicate your message so that it is understood. If someone doesn't get your message, they are not deliberately being annoying – it is merely feedback on how elegantly you deliver your communication.

Communicate With Clarity By Understanding Others

To maximize clarity, we must learn to deliver our message in a way that relates to the other person's view of the world. When you communicate, you also deliver your own beliefs and feelings through speech and body language. Become aware of these, and if possible keep them out of the way, so as not to pollute the communication with your views. Once you recognize that we all have different filters, you're able to be reasonable and easy-going when engaged in conversation. You gain skill in positioning the conversation to fit the other person's world so your message is clearly understood. The greater your understanding of how other people view the world, the more accurate you'll be with your communication, and the more often you'll get your desired outcome.

The Most Flexible Person Achieves Their Goal

Sometimes people get caught up in the emotion of the situation, instead of doing whatever it takes to ensure effective communication and therefore achieve their goal. For example, if someone's behavior becomes annoying, many people choose to grumble about the person, be condescending, or become forceful in their interaction. Close friends may terminate their friendship due to a misunderstanding, but this could be avoided if the other person's viewpoint was understood.

"Nothing is softer or more flexible than water, yet nothing can resist it."

Lao Tzu
(Chinese Taoist philosopher and founder of Taoism, 600–531 BC)

Some people are stubborn, and would rather wait for others to change. They may be unwilling to be flexible if they have an issue with the person and/or don't want the other person to gain from their actions. Rise above any thoughts of scoring points or gaining revenge, and focus instead on what is important – on what you want. The world is filled with people who are reluctant to be flexible. Those who are unwilling to be flexible miss out on achieving their goal.

It helps when you understand that people sometimes make what appear to be bizarre choices because they view life differently to you. Always keep the goal of the communication in mind. If it's important enough, it will be in your interests to choose a flexible attitude and change your communication to accommodate the other person. Always be prepared to do whatever it takes to communicate harmoniously and effectively. If you do that, you will become someone who always gets what you want.

Attracting Easy Communication

Once again, it is important to be aware of your thoughts and to select them carefully, because they attract people with those frequencies into your life; they are harmoniously attuned to you. Knowing what you want and creating goals attracts people who help you achieve your goals.

Always remain aware of your communication. You achieve greater results when you know it is up to you to ensure effective communication. Effective communication is a vital core competency every person should cultivate in order to get what they want.

Summary of

"Effectively Communicating with Others"

+ When you communicate with others it is up to you to accurately deliver the information.
+ We each live in a different reality because we filter our lives through our individual DNA, emotions, childhood, culture, and so on.
+ Most of us cannot be completely objective in any situation.
+ You must learn to deliver your message from the other person's point of view.
+ As you communicate, you deliver your own beliefs and feelings. You must endeavour to keep these out of the way.
+ The extent to which your message is understood reflects how elegantly it was delivered.
+ Always do whatever it takes to ensure effective communication. Alter the communication until it is clearly understood. Avoid getting emotional about it or giving up.
+ Keep the goal of the communication in mind, and remember that it is about getting what you want.
+ The more you understand about life and other people, the more often you will achieve your desired outcome.
+ Be willing to be flexible in your communication, as this increases the likelihood of achieving your goal. Allow others to benefit from your ability to be flexible.
+ Consciously choosing your thoughts and goals attracts people who will assist you on your path.

EXERCISE: How to Communicate Better

1. Whenever you communicate – either through speech or body language – it is with a purpose whether you are aware of the purpose or not. You may want to teach, give instructions, impress someone, calm them down or motivate them. By using effective communication, you can instantly achieve your goal.

2. We naturally get on with people who share our basic values and beliefs. To be assured of smooth communications with everyone, establish a relationship of friendliness and mutual trust by matching the tonality and speed of the person's voice (especially on the telephone), by matching some of their body language, and by matching their breathing. People who are like each other, like each other. Observe people in harmonious conversation – how they match each other's speech and body language. In the same way, if you wanted to end a conversation, you would 'mismatch' your communication with the other person.

3. Initially, match the other person's mood, and acknowledge what they are saying. Once you have a rapport developing, you can move to another topic of your choice.

4. Understand that most people are doing their best in a situation, and that there is usually a positive intention behind behavior. Avoid jumping to conclusions about other people's lives and intentions. Be sure to detect any feelings of arrogance or superiority you might have, and swap them with humility. Approach the person with a genuine aim to learn more about them, to understand them and to resolve the situation.

5. Avoid the use of the word 'but' – rather, use 'and'. You will still get your point across. For example, 'Overall, your handling of the project was excellent, *and* there are also a few areas you can improve on.'

6. Always be prepared to change your own behavior and remain humble to ensure successful communication.

7. Many aspects of this chapter are based on Neuro-Linguistic Programming (NLP). To further your skill in communication, invest in some books or courses on techniques such as NLP.

CHAPTER 8

Lose The Victim Mentality

"Be miserable or motivate yourself. Whatever has to be done is your choice."

Wayne Dyer
(American motivational speaker and author, b. 1940)

*A*lways do *whatever it takes*, with a light heart and courage, to find a solution to any challenge in your life. As with any challenge, finding solutions means taking responsibility, and puts you on a journey that opens you to new potentials.

Most People Indulge

The 'victim' label has unfavourable connotations for most of us, so this is an ideal time to leave behind *good* and *bad* and let it just *be* neither. If being a victim is too awful to consider, we may jeopardize our willingness to grow by pretending that it doesn't exist as part of our lives.

The victim mentality, often referred to as 'self-pity', 'poor me' or 'feeling sorry for oneself', is something we almost never admit to, either because we may not be conscious of doing it, or because of the social aversion to being a victim. Most men and women stoop to this behavior at least occasionally, so all of us should consider this as playing a part in our lives.

This chapter describes worst-case scenarios for the sake of clarity, but it varies in each of us, and is unlikely to be exhibited to this extent. Nevertheless, honesty is needed if you are going to detect anything that relates to you.

Generally, victims of self-pity feel that people don't understand them, and that life is against them. This can become addictive. Someone with a victim mentality will endeavour to keep life the same, because it provides justification for inadequacies in their life. This satisfies people for a while because it brings sought-after warmth, sympathy and attention, but there is no long-term satisfaction. Many victims of self-pity are angry at the world. They blame other people, are constantly suspicious, and belittle and criticize people.

The greater person is the one who can face it, and still love themselves. No one is perfect, and that part of you is still there, even if you ignore or hide it. Accepting and then mastering yourself is part of the journey. You only need to acknowledge it to yourself, and then you can move on to releasing it. Never allow anything to hold you back – not even you.

"This is my 'depressed' stance. When you're depressed, it makes a lot of difference how you stand. The worst thing you can do is straighten up and hold your head high because then you'll start to feel better. If you're going to get any joy out of being depressed, you've got to stand like this." Charlie Brown.
Charles M. Schulz
(American cartoonist of the comic strip 'Peanuts' 1922–2000)

Disguised Through Illness

A victim mentality takes many guises, and one of them is illness. As a rule, ill health guarantees more love and attention. We create every aspect of our lives, and some people unconsciously create accidents or illness to attract love and attention. Sometimes it just feels good to have an excuse to feel sorry for oneself. Allergies can also help people to feel unique. This is because people with allergies have to be treated specially and differently, and deep down, this attention feels good. This may be considered harsh and cruel, but if people are enlightened as to what is behind the ailment, such as a desire for love and attention, they can shift their mind towards a higher frequency and toward wellness. That's our goal, correct?

We give away our power when we seek love and attention in this way, because we are depending on someone else to satisfy our needs. It is a very inhibiting, limiting approach. Instead, we can break free from our shackles and give ourselves all the love and attention we want – we can create whatever we want in empowering ways. Of course, once we recognize the truth, we can launch ourselves to a greater life, as one does with all challenges.

When Maggie recovered from skin cancer, she used it as an opportunity to change her life. It was an easier change than it might have been, because she had a compelling reason to change. The cancer provided an excuse to change to a fulfilling job she had always longed to do and which allowed her more time with her children and husband.

While it's preferable to act prior to the onset of illness of course, recognize that challenges can assist you by providing excuses to create more freedom and your dream life.

Needing Protection Is *Not* an Asset

Low self-respect is another aspect of the victim mentality. If people cannot stand up for themselves and are constantly the victim of other people's demands, they use this as justification to feel sorry for themselves and complain. Acting weak and helpless can gain love and attention from other people, who may also empathize and offer protection. Once again, people who adopt the victim mentality refuse to take responsibility for their life, and remain powerless. A victim mentality is not an asset to anyone. Once a person identifies this in themselves and can recognize the consequences, their change of attitude will immediately lift and turn their life around. They will reach a point where they install appropriate boundaries for themselves and attract love and attention in more helpful ways.

Expecting Others to Take Care of Us

The victim mentality extends to the expectation that governments and corporations will provide us with all our needs. In many parts of the world, people expect governments to provide pensions for old age, and then complain that it is not enough. Certainly, we pay taxes, but are we the responsibility of the government? We are handing our power to the government when we say we can't look after ourselves. Standing back enables clarity, and we can then recognize our responsibility to cater for our old age. We should be grateful if the government provides anything at all. Likewise, many businesses now provide paid maternity leave, but this concept should be considered as a highly generous gesture, not as a basic right.

How can we expect to create independent, wonderful lives for ourselves if we hand over our power by expecting organizations to continually take care of us, and allowing them to determine how wealthy and happy we are?

"It is not the mountain we conquer, but ourselves."
Sir Edmund Hillary
(New Zealand mountaineer, who along with
sherpa Tenzing Norgay was the first man to reach
the summit of Mount Everest, 1919–2008)

The Addictive Cycle

It can be a challenge to turn away from a victim mentality, even for those who seldom rely on it. It is a survival strategy, and it is addictive. A tasty little crisis offers the opportunity to re-tell the story to friends, and receive extra attention, love and comfort in return. This is addiction, and it invariably means being trapped in a cycle of attracting issues so as to receive another hit of love from someone. Again, it means relying on someone else to provide what you want.

Acknowledge and Release It

Admitting it is powerful, and a relief, and is another step toward greater empowerment and increased self-esteem. We instantly gain awareness of these situations, and notice them for what they are. We may still be tempted, but we get better at sensing our motivations. Keep in mind that it is the body doing this, however, we intuitively know better, and have the power to change.

People are naturally drawn to inspirational conversation, rather than listening to constant complaints or descriptions of illnesses. They are drawn to strength and courage, and turned away by misery and apathy. A few complaints are acceptable as we search for an answer, but to repeatedly discuss the same problem or to continually have new problems is boring and annoying for friends and family. Recognize complaints for what they are – challenges and opportunities for growth. Friends and family are usually happy to support us in finding a solution, so we should use their help to put our new attitude into play and move on.

Elevating our attitude boosts our reality, even if we are still in the same situation, and it also allows other opportunities to appear.

Being an Asset to Yourself

Taking charge of your life through perseverance, determination and resilience quickly brings results. Previously, your issue seemed insurmountable, so you complained and said, 'Why me?' When you take charge, you expand your power, and by persisting, you find the answer. You feel stronger because you didn't give in, and you gain confidence by overcoming the body's fear.

Keep in mind, however, that we learn best through experience and if you have a strong urge to be a victim or to feel sorry for yourself, do it. Experience it; the urge means it is simply something you need for your learning. The knowledge you now have will motivate you to move on, something you must do to truly get what you want. All types of experience add to our wisdom and this applies to all aspects of this book such as taking responsibility, judging and blaming others etc.

Remember too, that books can only provide a certain amount of help. If you feel you need more help and support, seek it from someone who specializes in working with the mind. Do whatever it takes to live the most fulfilled life of your choosing.

Choosing the higher path is powerful and far more compelling than the scraps of love and attention you receive by being a victim. Taking charge means you are diligently selecting how your day will happen – your life does not happen haphazardly to you anymore, and you rely on yourself to make you happy and get what you want. You become a brilliant asset to yourself, and to the world.

Summary of

"Lose The Victim Mentality"

+ Do whatever it takes to find a solution to a challenge in your life.
+ Most people would never admit to being a victim, but most people have an aspect of it in their personality and exhibit that type of behavior in some way.
+ A person with a victim mentality feels like people don't understand, and that life is against them.
+ A victim mentality tries to keep life the same, as it is justification for inadequacies in life.
+ A victim mentality holds people back from achieving greatness in their lives.
+ Illness is a way for a person with a victim mentality to generate love and attention.
+ Being a victim can be addictive, as it is a way of finding love and attention.
+ Constant complaining is boring for others.
+ Recognize complaints as challenges, which are really opportunities.
+ Perseverance in solving problems brings results. Taking charge and persisting provides greater self-esteem and power. You are choosing the life you want.

EXERCISE: Moving On from Being a Victim

Example 1:
You need help from your partner with a situation that is bothering you, e.g. maybe you hardly spend any time together, or maybe you need their help with the children –

it can be any aspect of your life concerning your partner with which you aren't happy. With a few adjustments, this technique can be also be used at the office with colleagues.

1. Firstly, discuss changes or the need for help in a direct manner. This may sound obvious, but people often wait for their partners to volunteer assistance. If it hasn't happened yet, it won't happen. People may feel afraid of asking for help, as they're unable to predict the response.

2. People also say, 'But I've tried.' If you have tried, without any satisfaction, and you want to stand up for yourself and get a satisfactory result, here are some useful techniques to consider. This is best done in a calm manner, as little is accomplished through anger – you can achieve all that you want and more by handling the situation and the communication appropriately. Patience is also an asset. Remember, you have chosen and accepted this life until now, so give other people time to prepare for changes and become accustomed to your new attitude. Before we begin, note that you need to be motivated to make changes, or you won't want to put in the effort.

3. Start by considering small changes to alleviate the situation. Often, people want everything done immediately – they've had enough. It depends on whether you think the relationship is worth the patience.

4. Prepare for what you want to talk about. Consider your partner's life too, their feelings, their issues and how busy they are. Include this when you chat. Have some choices in mind so they have options in how they help, and be prepared to ask them if there is anything they would choose as a way of helping the situation. This is about creating balance in the relationship – so tell them that. This preparation starts the process toward finding a solution with your partner, because you are taking action by creating a goal, and already changing your thoughts.

5. Prepare your partner for the chat. You may want to suggest dinner at a restaurant, and tell them you would like to discuss a few things with them. Their curiosity will be piqued, and they'll probably say, 'About what?' Give a few hints as to the topics. Do this so that they don't feel ambushed. They are

now expecting the discussion, and realize that, as opposed to just a passing complaint, this is a serious discussion. They may even want to have the discussion immediately, and depending on your relationship, you may choose to do so. This is why I suggest preparing your discussion ahead of time. Dining out is preferable, as this means you are both relaxed, in a place of neutral energy and in an environment that is conducive to getting along.

6. When you have the chat, be as sensitive as possible, and never criticize – never be aggressive, accusing or arrogant. Keep your intentions pure, and be fair. Be humble without being submissive. Sometimes, people who haven't stood up for themselves can do a 180-degree turn and become the very thing they despised; they can start to dictate terms, or become a tyrant. You achieve more through sensitivity and working together than you do through demands and it is important that you keep your ultimate goal clear in your mind. If your intent is to score points through criticism, you won't achieve a positive long-term outcome. The aim is to resolve the situation as two responsible adults who care for each other, and who have a genuine desire to resolve the issue and strengthen the relationship.

7. At the dinner, remember that you are entitled to a balanced relationship. Therefore, when you speak, be focused and strong in your belief about what you are asking for. Ask your partner for ideas about resolving the situation. That enables them to take ownership of the issue. If you make suggestions, ask them if they agree with what you are proposing. Usually, by having pure intentions and being in an ideal environment you will gain agreement.

8. Occasionally, the partner agrees, but does not follow through with the agreement. This is highly unlikely if the discussion has been fair, understood by both partners, and they want the best for each other, but if it happens, don't let it deter you from your goal. Try another angle, or try to understand them better. They obviously didn't understand the earnestness of your request. If your partner is not following through, suggest a date for a future discussion to ask your partner if there is anything that is getting in the way of resolving

the issue, and once again ask them for ideas as to how to resolve the situation, and agree on a plan. Confirm that your partner can work with the proposed solution. Beyond this, you'll get more ideas by reading books on this topic, or you may consider seeking assistance from a third party, such as a relationship counselor.

Example 2:

You find yourself complaining about a lack of money. This topic is discussed further in the Chapter 17 on *Abundance*.

1. It's your attitude to money, rather than how much you actually have, that plays the most important role. To have more money, and to be confident with it, you need to have an ideal attitude toward money.
2. To achieve a desirable attitude, you need to gain knowledge such as you are presented with in this book. There are many other books available to help you achieve the thoughts and attitudes you need to attract money.
3. You already know that your thoughts create your reality. A poor person with an abundance mentality is wealthier than a rich person with a scarcity mentality. The person with the scarcity mentality will never feel that they have enough. That's why it is vital that we are conscious of our attitude, so we can enjoy today, rather than waiting for the future in order to have fun. Many people have more than enough money, but they fear the future, and are not conscious enough to live in the moment and enjoy it.
4. When we gain knowledge about an abundance mentality, we gain a feeling of power; the power to enjoy ourselves today, and to create anything we want in our lives.
5. If money is something that interests you, be willing to read books on the topic, learn about investing, etc. Again, the key is education, and taking action with the knowledge you have gathered to gain the experience that takes you to your desired outcome.

Example 3:

You would like to be healthy; to move on from colds, flu and other illnesses.

1. Using illness to help us feel better is probably ingrained in most people's DNA. Recognizing what is really going on is a powerful first step. We know it is possible to move from having several colds a year to never having one again – although small steps toward eliminating them is also progress.

2. Acknowledge that you now know there is more to illness. Ask yourself why you want attention, or what it is that you need to resolve, and then ask yourself to think of more helpful ways of achieving your goal.

3. It could mean several things – you may need a break from your daily routine, you may be unhappy in your job, you could be frustrated about something. Perhaps you need to spend more time with your partner, or perhaps it's an extra busy time for you; it could be anything. Contemplate what it is, so that you can either change the situation or change your attitude toward it. When we change our attitude, we change our thoughts.

4. Try to recognize the signs before illness strikes, and then act to alleviate the stress.

5. Acknowledge that radiant health is always a more rewarding option, and start changing your attitude to one that prefers being strong, powerful and healthy every day. Seek opportunities to ensure your happiness and health. When you have a challenging situation, choose to rise up and take action to resolve it, rather than sink into apathy or illness. When we see it for what it is, being ill is inconvenient and a burden, to ourselves and to others. The type of attention one gets from illness is not inspirational, whereas someone with a can-do attitude becomes a blessing and an inspiration, to themselves and to everyone else. They love themselves, and everyone else loves them as well. A person who actively tunes in to their needs, and acts on them, gains a long-term advantage in all areas of their life.

EXERCISE: Daily Attitudes to Stay Fulfilled

1. Decide to be courageous in all situations. You can create courage simply by changing your mind to form the

intention. When you see the words 'I am courageous' in your mind, your brain fires those neurons, and in that moment you are absolutely courageous. You can face anything. Create a few affirmations, such as, 'I am proud of my courage', 'I can solve any challenge', or 'Solutions magically appear especially for me.' Get creative, and have fun making some up for yourself. Even just creating the affirmations builds your confidence. Each situation you face with bravery and courage builds your ability, but it starts with that first step. Once you have attempted it, you will feel proud of yourself, and you'll walk taller – even more so if you create an awareness to notice the resulting benefits.

2. Try your best to recognize the value in everything. Be someone who is resilient, with a cheerful outlook on life, regardless of the current situation. Take some time each morning or evening to identify the wonderful aspects of your life. Most of us gloss over the most important and best parts of our lives. This is usually because it is the simplest aspects of our life that make us happiest, and we forget about them because they form the background to our life. The more you do this exercise, the more blessings you will detect in your life, and you will gain deep pleasure from acknowledging them. This easy exercise fills you with strength, happiness and faith for the moment, as well as for your future. There is more on this later in Chapter 16 on *Gratitude*.

3. If a situation moves off track or out of your control, try to remain focused on the belief that the ultimate result will be best for you. Even if you worry initially, refocus and imagine having every infinite potential for a wonderful result. Both attitudes take the same amount of energy, but only one ensures a great outcome.

4. If you feel trapped in a situation, with few options, choose to contemplate whether you have considered all your alternatives. Tell yourself there are alternatives you haven't considered, and that you are giving yourself some time to discover what they are. You must inform the body that there is more to this than you realize, and that the options will come to you (and they will). Over the next few days, you could

choose to be still and reflect, or you may find ideas coming to you as move about your day. You could also chat about the issue with a friend who likes finding new possibilities. It is vital that we explore our alternatives, because choice inspires us, and makes us feel like we're in control.

5.   Many people get trapped into putting their life on hold until their goal is realized, however they may get stuck in their progress toward the goal, and they miss all the potentials in the meantime. If you're in a situation that won't be resolved for a while, find value in the current situation. When we turn our minds away from waiting for the next step, and focus instead on what we can do today, we gain new insight into the situation, and can see the opportunities we already have. You may find things you can do in this situation that you won't be able to do so easily once you've achieved your goal. Enjoy the moment you're in.

6.   Investigate your areas of special interest. Take them a stage further, instead of wishing they were in your life. If you already have something you love doing, make an intention to structure your time to include more of it in your week. You'll feel worthwhile, happy, and gain greater belief that you can achieve anything.

7.   Eating well and drinking lots of water definitely lifts the spirits. While we enjoy our treats in the moment, the happy effects are gone the minute the last morsel disappears. Continued overindulgence in processed food becomes an addiction. Try to ensure that most of your main meals are wholesome, and of an appropriate size. You could also assess what issue snacking alleviates. How does it help you? Can you fulfil yourself in other ways? It could be boredom, sadness, low self-esteem, frustration, and so on. The more fulfilled we are, the less we think of food.

8.   Listen to uplifting music and surround yourself with laughter – through people, books or movies. Both music and laughter are extremely powerful frequencies and they instantly lift your life to an elevated level of fun and happiness.

9.   Try to include something that is special for you, and provides pure enjoyment, in every day. Map out and plan the hours of your week to ensure that you set aside time

for you. Get creative, and do whatever it takes to achieve that time. Your goal eventually is for your entire day to be special and fulfilled – each special moment for you counts toward that goal.

It is important to know that whatever the unhappy situation, we are always better off taking action to help ourselves. Settling for illness, unhappiness or constant complaining takes us away from our path and our purpose. It takes mental effort to make changes, but the rewards are rich. You can choose when the time is right to put in the work, and results can be achieved with only a little effort. Remember, you are here to live the best and happiest life possible.

Section 3

Paving the Way to What You Want

"He is able who thinks he is able."

Buddha

*Y*our life is yours to create, and you can create any dream you choose. You can choose happiness, sadness, wealth, poverty, health, illness…it's all done through your thoughts, and you are only limited by what you think you are entitled to. Do you think you are entitled to have it all? If you said 'yes', you're right. Only you can hold you back…and only you can decide to *have it all*.

Admittedly, some people have a tough start in life, but when you understand that the life you create is about the thoughts you choose, you have an exceptional opportunity. We are all born equal – in our beings and in our ability to create.

No one is superior to you, and no one is worth less. Everyone is entitled to happiness, and to live their dream. The universe is infinite, so there is *always enough of everything* for *everyone* to live their dream. If you can imagine it, you can have it. Someone with an abundance of money has the same importance as someone who has created poverty. Someone who has been to university is equal to someone who is illiterate. Everyone is at a different stage of development and in a different stage of wealth, love and awareness. The key is your growth as a person, not your ownership of a billion-dollar business. You are unique. If we all knew this, the world would be a happier place. There is no level playing field to compare us all. It matters only that, at our core, we are all pure love, and we all have the same power to create our lives as we choose.

Rise to your own ideals – greatness isn't achieved by doing what everyone else is doing. Is most of the world happy? No, so avoid following the masses. Quietly go your own way, listen to yourself and choose what interests you.

> *"Most folks are about as happy as they make up their minds to be."*
>
> Abraham Lincoln
> (Sixteenth President of the United States, 1809–1865)

The following chapters highlight areas that hold people back from achieving their dreams, and show you what to attend to in your life, so as to pave the way to *creating your dreams.*

CHAPTER 9

Living in Other People's Shadows

"If you don't design your own life plan, chances are you'll fall into someone else's plan. And guess what they have planned for you? Not much."

Jim Rohn
(American motivational speaker and author, b. 1930)

*M*any people build their lives based on other people's opinions, or on what they imagine others want from them. For most people, it's important that they be accepted by others. They haven't ever really considered their own needs and wants. Surely we can do better than that. To build a brilliant life, you need to follow *your own* soul and do what *you* love.

Say, 'No Thanks'

Living for someone else usually involves self-sacrifice. This is often done for approval, and is due to a lack of self-worth. Additionally, many religions and cultures have taught that self-sacrifice is admirable, that doing things for others is more significant than doing things for ourselves. It is considered virtuous, and a way of gaining acceptance.

Even though many people choose to live their lives through others, they unconsciously expect gratitude for sacrificing themselves. This sounds ridiculous, but it's done without awareness, however intuitively, they know they are being robbed, and they want something in exchange. Frustration and disappointment is the result, which in turn means someone gets blamed. On the flip side, people are more likely to appear ungrateful and disrespectful if they sense someone is sacrificing themselves. This is because they intuitively know self-sacrifice is not worthy of respect.

If you are living your life for or through someone else, you have not been forced to do so. You are robbing yourself, and you have elected to do so. Instead, keep it clean, and live your life for *you.*

> "Be a first rate version of yourself, not a second rate version of someone else."
>
> Judy Garland
> (American actress and singer, 1922–1969)

Giving With No Strings Attached

If you help someone or give something, never expect gratitude – do it out of love, and because you feel empowered to do so. Otherwise, don't do it.

When you are fulfilled and empowered, you never need gratitude and you never expect it. Your goal is *not* approval from others. Help others with a free spirit, so the need for gratitude fades away. Do it when you are vibrant, aware and grateful for your life, and feeling good about yourself. You can then assist others as a conscious choice with a generous free spirit. Avoid self-sacrifice. When you help others with a free and open heart, you receive gratitude and approval anyway.

Sometimes, we need to serve others prior to being ready to do it willingly, such as in a family situation. This can be difficult, but is part of the journey toward inner power. The key in a family is balance for all concerned. Even as you are learning to take responsibility for your life and to create your dream life, you and your family should strive for mutual respect.

"Living with integrity means: Not settling for less than what you know you deserve in your relationships. Asking for what you want and need from others. Speaking your truth, even though it might create conflict or tension. Behaving in ways that are in harmony with your personal values. Making choices based on what you believe, and not what others believe."

Barbara De Angelis
(American researcher on relationships and personal growth)

Stand Tall – Let Yourself Shine

Needing or seeking approval from others takes you away from your ideal path. If there is an aspect of life you are interested in learning about, no one has the right to stop you. Always feel free to explore life in the way you choose. It is common to want approval from our family or friends before starting a course or new avenue in life, but bravely break the shackles and trust yourself to know what is right for you. In some cultures, the pressure to conform is tremendous. You need to be determined and courageous to go for what is important to you, and what makes you happy. By all means, discuss your interests with your family. Ask their opinion and consider it, but ensure you still make the final decision, and that it makes you happy.

Stand tall and firm, and be yourself. Let yourself shine. Show a quiet strength. People are drawn to strength, and turned away by weakness and desperation. You are unique and special – admire the contribution you make to the world, and make your life count. You are here to do the exceptional – for you.

Summary of

"Living in Other People's Shadows"

♦   When people live through others, it is because they want acceptance from others, and haven't seriously considered what they want in their lives.

♦   Many of these people expect gratitude for their self-sacrifice.

♦   If you are living your life through others, you have chosen to do so.

- Many religions and cultures teach that self-sacrifice is admirable, however we should only serve others when we can do it freely, without the need for gratitude.
- Sometimes, our dreams affect our family and friends, and they don't approve. In some cultures, the pressure to conform is tremendous. You always have the option to follow your dream.
- Always feel free to explore life without needing the approval of others.

EXERCISE: How to Make Your Life Count

Example:

Living your partner's life.

1. More commonly, it is the wife who sacrifices her life for those of her husband and children, but many husbands also over-sacrifice.

2. People are usually unaware they are living this type of life, and are also unaware of other options. That's fine, if you are happy, but if you are dissatisfied or frustrated and ready for a greater life, then you should do something about it. By not doing anything about it, people may encounter illness, challenges, depression, etc.

3. You can get what you want without needing to involve your partner. You may want pity or attention from your partner, but what you really want is a long-term solution. You need to contemplate what you want for you, and decide how to achieve it.

4. Do what it takes to get what you want. If you need help taking action, seek a supportive friend who is objective and of high integrity. This person's role is to encourage you, and to help you follow through.

5. Gently stretch your comfort zone. Start to do things that interest you, and which don't require discussion with your partner. This is also a test as to whether it is pity we want or a better life. If taking action is too much effort, then it is pity we want (but remember, the gratifying effects of pity are short-term, and not empowering, because you rely on others

to provide it). We should also remember that someone who takes care of themselves and stands up for what is best for them is a far more interesting partner.

6. Endeavour to reach a point where you feel as important and as happy as the rest of the family. The more you love yourself, the more love you will have for your family.

7. This technique works for any situation where you are living someone else's life instead of your own. The secret is to do whatever it takes to make you happy, rather than relying on gaining happiness via other people.

CHAPTER 10

Set Yourself Free
From Obligation

"Relationships based on obligation lack dignity."

Wayne Dyer
(American motivational speaker and author, b. 1940)

*A*s children, most of us were encouraged to put others
first. It is time to put up your hand and say, 'STOP…that's
enough!' The issue of obligation can be subtle, puzzling, tough to
handle and frustrating, because it distracts you from achieving
your own dreams.

Obligation Obstructs You From Getting What You Want

You throw away your power and freedom of choice when
you act out of obligation. People whose lives are immersed in
obligation constantly put other people's lives ahead of their own.
Obligation affects most of us, yet it often remains unnoticed. It
can easily become a large part of our lives, and can contribute
to ill health, since self-sacrifice has replaced self-love and self-
importance. If obligation is a big part of your life, you definitely
won't be getting what you want in life.

No Fun? It's Obligation

The first step is to spot obligation, and while this can be
tricky, a clue is when you feel no sense of fun and excitement

in your activities. Obligation makes you feel tired, drained and frustrated. Have you recently found that you'd rather be doing something else, or be somewhere else, but you feel you have no choice? Many people even feel obliged to be in their job, which is hard to believe, since that is where they spend most of their time.

Respecting Your Own Feelings Benefits Others

The more you honor yourself, the less obliged you will feel to others, the less frustration you will experience and the more your life will flow. Doing what *you* want to do helps circumstances fall into place. We are all created equal, so you are entitled to do what you want to do, just as the next person is entitled to do what's right for them. Others benefit when you are fulfilled, because you're more patient and understanding, and you have more love to give. As you honor yourself, so you lift your self-belief and self-love. You are rewarded, as you give yourself the attention and love you deserve (and, by default, then receive these things from others, too).

Feeling the Pressure to Please Others

So, what do you do when someone asks you a favour and you find yourself feeling pressured? You may feel awkward saying no, nevertheless, you are entitled to do so. This is a skill that can be learned, if you are willing. If you are feeling obliged, rather than pleased to participate, then honor that feeling – it is the only reason you need to say no. We usually try to find justification for our unwillingness, but you are entitled to say no without a 'tangible' reason. You intuitively know what is best for you, and you should trust that intuition. Guilt can appear at this stage, but resist paying attention – this is a belief by the body that being liked and accepted by others is more important than getting what you want. The body feels troubled if it thinks it is annoying others.

"Be who you are and say what you feel because those who mind don't matter and those who matter don't mind."

Dr. Seuss
(American writer and cartoonist, 1904–1991)

This may not be easy if you have always worried about what others think, and whether they will still like and accept you. Start small. Often, change isn't comfortable, but it's time to put some faith in yourself and break away from what others think. Remain focused on your entitlement to happiness, and toss out the need for approval from others. Approval from others does not supply you with long-term happiness.

Setting Boundaries for Requests

Some people take advantage of others, and if you haven't learnt to say no, you'll find yourself doing what others want. If you allow others to dictate your life you give away your power and put your life in their hands. Even if you initially say yes and regret it, you still have the right to withdraw. You should cancel if your heart isn't in it. If you say yes when you mean no, you are being dishonest with yourself and with others, and you are telling yourself that other people's needs are more important. This causes a deep sense of dissatisfaction.

While out walking one day I saw my friend Emma. Her youngest child had recently started school, and she was enjoying her freedom. I fondly remembered my own freedom after several years of babies and toddlers, but I noticed that Emma was looking after another toddler, and she looked unhappy. I learned that the toddler belonged to a woman Emma had just met at her school. Emma had felt obligated to look after the child, because the child's mother had asked her for a favour. She'd been asked to look after the child two days a week for several weeks, and now she looked frustrated. She hadn't been able to say no, and was filled with regret. Emma expected others to recognize when a request is inappropriate, so that she wouldn't have the ordeal of saying no.

"Don't be trapped by dogma - which is living with the results of other people's thinking. Don't let the noise of others' opinions drown out your own inner voice. And most important, have the courage to follow your heart and intuition. They somehow already know what you truly want to become. Everything else is secondary."

Steve Jobs
(Apple co-founder, b. 1955)

Avoid doing things for other people that you don't want to do, and avoid going to places you'd rather not. Saying no takes practice. The first time is the hardest. Usually, the person will be disappointed, but will not necessarily be annoyed with you. If you genuinely feel entitled to say no, they will instantly understand, but if they do get nasty, let them handle that issue. Be understanding as they cope with the disappointment.

Harmony for You Means Harmony for All

Obligation is a subtle area, and wisdom develops with experience. Usually, when you follow what is appropriate for you, it also creates the best result for others, even in minor situations, as the following story attests.

I was invited to a friend's for lunch. It was a busy week, and when the day arrived I felt overwhelmed, and was annoyed that I had agreed to lunch. Even though I felt uneasy, I decided to call my friend to let her know I couldn't make it for lunch, only to find that she had a cold and was feeling dreadful. She was so relieved that I had called to cancel. (Of course, ideally, she should also have felt entitled to cancel.)

Again, it depends on the circumstance as to whether you follow through on your agreement, but in most situations, you should follow your truth. It simplifies your life.

Step Lightly Be Gentle

As always, you'll need motivation to step into a new mindset. The people you are dealing with probably still believe you should put others (them) first. They may also be used to your undivided attention. Once they recognize that they can also do what is right for them, they have an opportunity to enjoy the benefits as well.

Be gentle, compassionate and understanding if others are confused or hurt, because you are changing. As you take care of yourself, be strong in the knowledge that honoring yourself is an important part of getting what you want, that you are worth it and that they will be fine. As you adjust, they do too. By stepping into the unknown of standing up for yourself, you get to experience and understand it and your brain settles into the new pattern. It now senses and understands the new you. Give this a chance.

If people still don't understand, despite your gentle approach, then hard as it is, you must allow them to live their lives and let them discover what they need to learn. They, too, have their areas in which they need to evolve. Some of them may drift away from you. If you trust yourself to continue, you will find new, inspiring people entering your life. They will be happy, confident people who also honor themselves. They will match the new you, and there will be no sense of obligation.

It is your responsibility to live your life in the most brilliant way you can, but it is an imposition to attempt to get others to do so as well. Their life is also sacred, and they may not be ready for growth. If you interfere, you may inadvertently hinder their growth.

One Day at a Time and You Get There

These ideas may seem strange at first, but the understanding comes from trying them out. As you integrate the experience, the concept becomes real, and you'll understand the value in thinking this way. Initially, do something every day that makes you happy, something where there is no obligation involved...just pure happiness for yourself. Keep that up, and one day your entire day will be what you want. There is no need for you to examine how this happens – the enchanting quantum field and your magnetic power will take care of it.

You Will Always Help... on Your Terms

Of course, as with anything in life, you need to keep a balance. It's in our nature to help others, and mostly, you will continue to do so, sometimes because you feel you have to. Keep tabs on this balance. Help others, but preferably not to your detriment. You'll develop the ability to be discerning and ensure equilibrium in your life. Once you've said no the first time, you'll say it less often, because your boundaries will be set, and you won't feel indebted to others. If a situation arises, you may still choose to do it, but you will have grown in this area, and you won't be allowing others to dictate your life. You'll be taking charge. When this happens, you will be ready to volunteer your time in ways you choose.

Remember, most people will respect you more and want to be around you because you now respect and like yourself. This will always be the result, but with changes such as this, you firstly need the courage to be prepared to lose it all...so that you can have it all. You'll only have this courage when you feel worthy of standing up for yourself.

Always ensure that your life brings you joy and fun. Your greatest gains, and the greatest benefits for others, will be achieved on this path.

Like Magic

When you implement this attitude and, even better, when you genuinely recognize the advantages of this attitude, others will simply accept it, and you will attract people who support you in this thinking. This is because they mirror your thoughts.

Trust that your new way of thinking will attract people and circumstances to your life to confirm your actions, encourage you, and help you achieve this task of releasing obligation. You are clearing the way to achieving your greatest potentials.

Summary of

"Set Yourself Free From Obligation"

♦   To be obligated is to lose freedom of choice. Anyone participating in obligation has moved off the path of their dreams.

♦   Obligation causes you to feel tired, ill and frustrated, and there is no sense of fun.

♦   You are entitled to do what you want to do, and what makes you happy.

♦   If a request makes you feel pressured or obligated, you are entitled to say no. The guilt we feel is because we have been taught to put others first, and then we feel exposed, because the body considers it dangerous to annoy people.

♦   Even if we initially say yes, we have the right to withdraw.

♦   Saying no is hardest the first time, but after you've done it once, you won't attract these situations as much.

- Start understanding the feeling of obligation to help you learn what is best for you.
- Start with small situations, so you can gently get used to choosing what you want, and be less concerned about what others think of you.
- If others can't accept the new you, keep going and allow them to use that as an opportunity for their growth. Continue to remind yourself of your entitlement to have what you want and to be happy.
- It's in our nature to help others, and once you have retrieved your power, you develop a healthy balance when doing so.

EXERCISE: How to Avoid Obligation

1. When people need help, whether this becomes apparent in a group discussion or one-on-one, you can offer to help if it is something you really want to do. If you feel obligated, i.e. pressured or uncomfortable, then stay silent or find another way to help, a way that is more enjoyable to you. Listen to the whispers of your soul. If a part of you is reluctant, you should listen; it is reluctant for a good reason. You may feel a twinge of guilt at this stage, but this twinge is easier to handle than the feelings of frustration you'd have for putting yourself in an unhappy situation. Be aware, too, of your motivation when you offer help. Are you doing it from a genuine desire to help, or are you hoping to receive gratitude or friendship? Help others for the right reasons. Be assured, if you don't help, there will always be someone else who can help them – it doesn't always have to be you. By standing back, you create a window for someone else to step in. In any case, allow others to be responsible for their lives; you don't have to hover around them all the time to make sure all is well.
2. Even if you genuinely want to help, always be sure you understand what is involved, as it could entail more than you realize.

3. Remember at all times that not only are you are entitled to choose what you do, it is essential that you do so. Keep in mind that your love for yourself comes first.

Different Ways of Responding to a Request:

Always do your best to say what you are feeling, and be honest. Sometimes, we have an inner voice, our soul, screaming 'no' for a variety of reasons – perhaps you have another commitment, or the favour that has been asked will result in something you resent doing. Listen to your soul.

Although it can be difficult, it's always best to tell the truth, but if you struggle with being direct with people, here are some answers you can give:

♦ 'Tell me what's happening….' This buys you time to think.
♦ 'I'm not sure right now…I'd rather not answer yet…let me get back to you.' This allows you to avoid being pressured into an immediate yes.
♦ 'Saying no is difficult for me….' If it is, be honest. Usually, we feel bad about not helping, it feels selfish (by the way, there's no such thing) and it can be hard to put ourselves first, so it's okay to say that you're having difficulty saying this.
♦ 'That's a tough situation, however….' Again, if you think it is, be honest. Empathize with the person, but still only do what you want to do.

If you are someone who has trouble saying no, then assess the situations in which you most often find yourself. Start off with the most common situation, so that you can be ready with a response.

If No is Unavoidable and You Are

Feeling Trapped

While the best way is to tell the truth, if this is proving too challenging for you, try the following, delivered in a suitable tone of voice, to express reluctance. This will help convey your message and it at least gets you onto the page of doing what you want. To get you started, use any means possible to *avoid getting involved* in something where you feel obligation. It's not worth it, because it will not provide you with what you want (long-term).

'I can help for a short time...'

'I can help this time...'

'Let's chat about some solutions....'

Practice getting to a stage where you always say and do what you want. You want friendships where you are allowed to say no without persecution, where everyone is allowed to do what they want. How refreshing. But it starts with you – you're the one who makes this happen.

CHAPTER 11

Choosing an Unlimited Viewpoint For Your Life

"Let others lead small lives, but not you. Let others argue over small things, but not you. Let others cry over small hurts, but not you. Let others leave their future in someone else's hands, but not you."

Jim Rohn
(American motivational speaker and author, b. 1930)

Choice means freedom. Before making decisions, try to find and explore several options. There are usually other alternatives, and sometimes all that is required is the intention to find them. It's important to find as many as you can. We're more likely to fall into a trap of hopelessness and self-pity in a difficult situation if we feel there is only one option.

Add to Your Choices

Health is so important, and it is an ideal way to illustrate limited viewpoints. Doctors play an important role, and provide an excellent service to humanity, but their influence means they can tell people virtually anything and be believed. Be alert and aware, otherwise you might inadvertently accept an unhelpful or even incorrect diagnosis. Ask yourself if it serves you to accept this view, and whether there is possibly another solution. There are always several options, even if they are not immediately obvious. Anything is possible.

Our orthodontist wanted to extract two baby teeth from my eight-year-old son's mouth. I was told that this was the only option, and that I was delaying the inevitable, as they were blocking his emerging adult teeth. The day came when our orthodontist said we should make an appointment with the dentist to remove the teeth. I was uncomfortable putting my son through that, and felt there must be another way. The next day, we went to the movies, and there in the advertisements was a new technology that straightens children's teeth without braces and – yes, you guessed it – without extractions.

Avoid Premature Conclusions

If you visit your doctor with an unusual ailment, ask them to avoid coming to any premature conclusions, and especially to avoid mentioning any gloomy suspicions to you. Although the symptoms of an ailment may at first seem serious, it often turns out to be minor. A doctor told a friend of mine it seemed likely that she had a terminal illness. Understandably, the entire family went into a state of panic, but tests subsequently revealed that the ailment was trivial.

Even though your mind can overcome any illness, it is best to avoid troubling it with unnecessary concerns. Friends and family can quickly move to doom and gloom, and pass on the sad prognosis to their network. Many people love a drama, but it's best to avoid linking a serious disease to anyone, the reason being that our thoughts are powerful, and if several people are imagining a friend to be sick...mmm...you work it out.

"If you limit your choices only to what seems possible or reasonable, you disconnect yourself from what you truly want and all that is left is compromise."

Unknown

Beware the Common Ailment – Dare to Challenge It

When a label is accepted as commonplace, e.g. asthma or eczema, people are more likely to unwittingly slide into accepting it. How about contemplating the validity of the diagnosis, or considering another solution? This is different from being in denial. Choose to research whether anyone has ever overcome this issue. Chances are they have, but it may not be widely known. Why not choose to be the first person to overcome the ailment? Every step you take to overcome it adds to your wisdom, something you keep forever. Every ounce of effort is worth it, even if you don't find anything. Nothing is ever wasted. Any unwelcome diagnosis is a signal to search deeper, and to commence a journey in a new direction.

At best, you may find that it isn't what you thought, and at worst, along the way you'll make fresh discoveries about yourself, your life and your body. Even if, for now, you need to treat an ailment in the prescribed manner, never stop trying to find ways to overcome it. Never accept it. If you accept it, then it will certainly be true.

In many cases, the better you understand your life, body and mind, the more you can completely avoid doctors and find answers in other ways, no matter what the issue. The mind is always capable of achieving radiant health, because the body follows the thoughts, without question.

"No one is in control of your happiness but you; therefore,
you have the power to change anything about yourself or
your life that you want to change."

Barbara De Angelis
(American researcher on relationships and personal growth)

Alternatives Are Available and Miracles Do Happen

There is plenty of reading material dedicated to thousands of miraculous healings. If you have access to the Internet, a simple search will provide you with plenty of examples. Many alternative healing methods such as naturopathy, homeopathy, kinesiology, the Feldenkrais method, qigong, reiki, and so on, are available to support you on your journey of healing. Always research your choice of healing and practitioner thoroughly prior to having treatment. This not only protects you, but also raises your levels of acceptance/belief to create a greater outcome.

Accept Only Your Ideal Future

Choose unlimited viewpoints in all areas of your life. We've all heard the stories of teachers telling a student they won't amount to much, and yet the student grows up to make a beautiful difference in the world, proving that anyone can achieve their dreams. Ignore other people's opinions of you and choose to be whatever you want to be, and to get whatever you want.

Prick up your ears if you hear, 'You can't…', 'You'll never be able to do that', or 'That's impossible.' Your attitude should be, 'I am able to do anything I choose.' Any challenge can be overcome, starting with a can-do attitude.

Avoid accidentally handing over your future to someone else. If you think you can overcome a situation, you can. Miracles will happen for you. As you build awareness, brick by brick, you'll develop the ability to snap to attention when someone else is limiting your potential.

If you have an intention to accept only the best answer for you, the quantum field will supply you with the ideas, people and circumstances to support that result. The key is perseverance and belief that the answer is there. Unlock your potential, and you will be free to have it all.

Summary of

"Choosing an Unlimited

Viewpoint For Your Life"

♦ Always add options before making a decision.
♦ Any time you feel cornered, with only one option, you should recognize it as a limited viewpoint.
♦ If you have an unusual ailment, ask the doctor to avoid coming to a premature conclusion. The premature conclusion may be more hazardous to you than the ailment. The brain can get trapped into believing it, and inadvertently create the issue in the body.
♦ Before accepting a label for an ailment, search for answers in other areas. Even if you have to take medication in the meanwhile, never give up searching for an answer long-term.
♦ Be aware of anyone saying you can't do something, or you don't have a choice. Never allow anyone to limit you.

♦   Choose to accept only the best answer for you, and it will be provided.

NOTE:

The exercises at the end of the next chapter, Chapter 12, *Making Your Own Decisions*, will help you develop greater viewpoints.

CHAPTER 12

Making Your
Own Decisions

"You have your way, I have my way. As for the right way, the correct way and the only way, it does not exist."

Friedrich Nietzche
(German classical scholar, philosopher and cultural critic,
1844–1900)

*Y*our magnificent life grows wings when you make your own decisions. Many people believe others know what is best for them, but only you know what is best for you.

Research is Always Valuable

When making a decision, continue to search until an answer appears that feels ideal for you. Research your options extensively, and feel free to discuss the issue with friends. Tell friends that you are only asking their opinion, so that you retain the freedom to make the ultimate decision. You may find yourself journeying on a convoluted path in search of the answer, only to find that a simple answer was there in front of you all along. This doesn't mean you wasted your time…you never waste time. The knowledge you gain along the way is priceless.

"We learn more by looking for the answer to a question and not finding it than we do from learning the answer itself."

Lloyd Alexander
(American author, b. 1924)

My daughter was old enough to start riding her bicycle to her best friend's house two streets away, and I assumed she knew the way, as we'd driven and walked it heaps of times. My daughter always got there and home safely on her bike and rather enjoyed her new freedom, but one day, while we were taking our dog for a walk around the suburb, she saw the streets in a new light, and exclaimed that she had been going completely out of her way to get to her friend's house.

I thought this was a great analogy for life. Life doesn't have a road map, so how often do we go the long way around to achieve a goal?

Risk a Mistake – There is No 'Wrong' Decision

"Promise me you'll always remember: You're braver than you believe, and stronger than you seem, and smarter than you think." Christopher Robin to Pooh.

A.A. Milne
(English humorist and creator of Winnie the Pooh, 1882–1956)

Your final answer may not necessarily be obvious, especially when your decision affects other people in your life, but it is still your responsibility to decide. If you let others decide for you, you'll have to stand by that choice, because you *chose* to let someone else make the decision. This is not empowering, in fact it is self-deprecating. Further, you now know that you can't blame someone else if the result isn't what you wanted.

Now, making your *own* decisions has an element of risk – you may be making a *mistake*! Many people, both adults and children, still find it awful to make mistakes, yet this is typically the way we learn. You are more powerful when *you* make the decisions, even if they take you in an unexpected direction.

"Forget about the consequences of failure. Failure is only a temporary change in direction to get you straight for your next success."

Denis Waitley
(American motivational speaker, b. 1933)

There is no such thing as a 'wrong' decision, because these provide guidance as you continue to look at different options and act on different possibilities. People naturally move toward improving themselves. The more decisions you make and actions you take, the more this ability grows, and the more confident you become. It is only by taking action that you discover your options. Taking any action is always better than being frozen in fear. No decision and no action is also a 'choice' you make. There is still a result…which you created.

Be Brave and Jump In

To really live the full, empowered life of your dreams, you'll need to step off the edge into the unknown. Start with small decisions. Remember – baby steps. When you do, and you're conscious about your thoughts, you will find that life has a way of supporting you. Your conscious thoughts attract appropriate situations and suitable people when you need them.

"Chaotic action is preferable to orderly inaction."

Will Rogers
(US humorist and showman, 1879–1935)

Simply… is the Best

Look for a straightforward solution. The best solution is usually the simplest one, or one that simplifies your life. It may not be what everyone else wants, but it is the simplest for *you*. These solutions are usually more aligned with your path. If an answer seems complicated, it's a good clue to look further. Be open to alternatives, or to different timing; delay the answer until you have considered all the options. Ideal answers have a harmony about them, even if they take you in a new direction, or decision making is new to you.

Only You Know Your Answer

You may need to be prepared to break away from what is considered normal, or what family and friends would expect from you. You are a unique human being with your own unique answer. More opportunities and insights usually lie within that answer.

Always respect yourself, consider your needs as sufficiently special to warrant your full attention, and know that you have the best answer for you. *Your* answer is the one that opens the doors of opportunity.

Summary of
"Making Your Own Decisions"

♦   If you want to create your dream life, start making your own decisions. Only you know what is best for you.

♦   Put in the effort to search for an answer that feels right for you.

♦   If you let someone make a decision for you and you regret the result, remember that it was still your 'decision'.

♦   There is no such thing as failure. You gain knowledge and experience in everything you do, and this is priceless.

♦   Start with small decisions. Gently stretch yourself, and you will see that life supports you as you try.

♦   Simple, straightforward solutions are best. Complicated solutions are usually a sign to keep searching.

♦   Ensure your decision is what you want, and not what family and friends want or expect.

EXERCISE: How to Make Your Own
Decisions and Create a Greater Viewpoint

Use Technique 1 or 2 for everyday decisions such as deciding whether to drive or take a train to work (see example), whether to stay at home to care for your children, get a job, get a new job, stay in the current one, and so on. If you find yourself in a greater dilemma whereby you are in a challenging situation with great implications, use Technique 2. Technique 1 can also help, but it depends on the issue.

Technique 1 – PMI – Plus Minus Interesting

(This exercise is based on the work of author Edward de Bono, from his book *Serious Creativity*. This technique is outlined on the website www.mindtools.com.)

While this technique assists decision making, it also expands your view on the issue, helping you to discover new ideas and alternatives, and to know what you really want to do. Previously, people used a pros and cons approach, but this is an improvement on that. This develops your thinking flexibility, and teaches you to feel in control of situations. It also moves you toward removing your beliefs from the situation. Firstly, tell yourself you are open to considering alternatives and other viewpoints. Being open to new ideas is a key to becoming more objective with your life.

In the 'Plus' column, enter the positive outcomes of what you are considering.

In the 'Minus' column, enter all the problems or concerns you have.

In the 'Interesting' column, enter the unknown potentials or possible consequences of what you are considering. These may be helpful (positive), a hindrance (negative), or not known.

By this stage of your analysis, you may have already made your decision. Your decision does not necessarily have to 'add up' – this technique merely adds clarity to your options and assists your inner knowing. If you are still undecided, go through each point you made and allocate a positive or negative score (out of 5) depending on how much it affects you.

Total the scores. A positive score indicates you should take the action. A negative score means you should avoid it.

In the following example, a man is deciding whether he should start taking the train to work.

He scores the table as 20(Plus) - 15 (Minus) + 10 (Interesting) = +15

For him, it is more beneficial to travel to work by train than by car. He may still choose to drive in if he needs to be home at a certain time, or if he has an after-hours social engagement that is not near the train line.

Plus	Minus	Interesting
No traffic concerns (+5)	Trains may be delayed or cancelled (–3)	May be able to catch train with partner (+4)
Time to read the paper (+5)	Seating may be limited (–2)	Car parking issues at the train station (–2)
Time to study a new interest (+3)	Possibly late home (–2)	Time waiting on the platform (–3)
Time to review work documents (+3)	Reduced flexibility (–3)	Complete extra work on the train prior to coming home (+3)
Time to rest and listen to music or contemplate (+4)	Less control over time of departure (–2)	Relaxed already on the train prior to coming home (+3)
	Too many people on the train (–2)	Possibly less time at home (–4)
	Possibly late for appointments (–1)	Reduced flexibility for after-hours engagements (–2)
		Better for the environment (+5)
		Reduces traffic congestion in the city (+3)
		Still able to use the car when needed (+3)
+20	-15	+10

Technique 2

If you trust yourself, you will always have the best answer for you, but if you are not ready to make a major decision without help, then it's best to discuss your situation one-on-one with several friends or colleagues. This will help you to gain clarity, but make sure you only use them for that reason. Keep an open mind, and tell yourself that you are the one who must make the ultimate decision.

1. Choose people carefully. Choose people who are known for recognizing possibilities and alternatives.
2. Find people who have no vested interest in your decision, and who are willing to be objective and honest in their opinions.
3. Through discussion and hearing different viewpoints, you will become clear on what you want, and will uncover issues to consider.
4. You may discover that what you want isn't popular with others. This is quite common, but remain determined to do what is best for you.
5. The path may be a long one if it is a major dilemma you face. If so, re-visit your friends as you progress along the path. Sometimes, you can only make small decisions along the way, but these may change the situation, and each stage needs to be reassessed.
6. You will find yourself able to explore several options, but ultimately, you have the freedom to decide for yourself.

NOTE:

The first time you decide to make your own decisions, you may not settle on an answer immediately, but you will discover new avenues to investigate that will help you make a decision. Sometimes there are several aspects that need to be understood before you are ready to make a decision. It is all progress toward that decision. Relax into the process. It can be tempting to want the answer immediately, but if you want it to be your decision, and something that is ideal for you, go within. By stilling the mind and having the intention to find the best answer, you are already most of the way there.

CHAPTER 13

Friendships – Helping You or Holding You Back?

"The next best thing to being wise oneself is to live in a circle of those who are."

C. S. Lewis

(Author, Chronicles of Narnia, 1898–1963)

Inspiring people lift us up, make our journey fun and exciting, and help carry us even closer to our dream. Be deliberate about surrounding yourself with inspiring people. Avoid gatherings that involve talk of judging others, problems, complaining or going over the past...again and again. Participating in gossip attracts unpleasantness to you, and it also drags down the quality of your thoughts.

Putting Yourself Down Does Hurt You

Putting ourselves down has become a natural and 'fun' part of conversation with our friends, with comments like, 'No, I'm worse than that', or 'Sometimes I can't even remember my own name.' Many people are unaware of the damage this causes, both to them and to their dream. Initially, it can seem like a challenge to find a topic of conversation that doesn't involve problems, gossip or the past, but try anyway.

Become aware of 'throw-away' lines when you are with friends, because they can also take you away from your chosen future, for example, 'I nearly died', 'I could kill myself', 'I'm such an idiot', 'Why does this always happen to me?', 'I never win anything', 'I'll never afford that.' The body doesn't know the difference – it believes these words, and feels powerless when these statements are voiced. Voicing a harmful thought once has little effect, but when we litter our lives with similar sentences, they become our main focus and we attract them into our lives. Throw away the throw-away lines.

"You must constantly ask yourself these questions: Who am I around? What are they doing to me? What have they got me reading? What have they got me saying? Where do they have me going? What do they have me thinking? And most important, what do they have me becoming? Then ask yourself the big question: Is that okay? Your life does not get better by chance, it gets better by change."

Jim Rohn
(American motivational speaker and author, b. 1930)

You'll be able to tell if you are with an inspiring person, because the conversation instantly leads to ideas of potential and possibility. You'll feel motivated and encouraged – confident that you can achieve anything. When you are new to higher ways of thinking, you need support to keep thinking that way. Being around inspiring people does just that.

The Purpose of Friendships
Friendships are meant to come and go. Friendships have a purpose, and they should only continue as long as they are inspirational for both people. It is possible to have inspiring friendships that last a lifetime, but many friendships are transitory, and gradually diminish once the specific purpose has been fulfilled. By this point, you'll usually find yourself feeling drained of energy after each conversation.

Move on Once a Friendship is Over – Some Do End
Letting go of a friendship can feel odd. Humans have a history of being reluctant to let go, because letting go is like the death of a part of oneself, so letting go of a friendship can seem

heartless and ungrateful. You may even be concerned that with such an attitude, you'll have no friends! Instead, this attitude of freedom means that once a friendship is complete and the purpose is fulfilled, another inspiring friend can arrive for both of you. Yes, for *both* of you.

Moving on is essential to allowing this to happen. Staying in a friendship where you feel obligated blocks the arrival of new friends. Never allow obligation to drive a friendship. Your friends wouldn't like it if they knew you would rather be somewhere else. Let the friendship diminish over a period of time. Letting go allows the quantum field to work its magic so you can attract a new friends and allow them to arrive into your life. In this way, you will always have an abundance of inspiring friends.

By doing this, and by once again leaving obligation out of your life, you allow for the highest good of all concerned, and you gather friends who motivate and support you in your quest for a superb life.

Summary of "Friendships –

Helping You or Holding You Back?"

♦   Intentionally surround yourself with inspirational people.
♦   Putting yourself down – even playfully – limits your potential.
♦   'Throw-away' lines take you from your path, and your body can be harmed because your brain believes them.
♦   Inspirational people talk of potential and possibility.
♦   Friendships have a purpose, and should continue only as long as they remain inspirational. Friendships based on obligation lack purpose and make us feel drained of energy.
♦   Learn to let go of friendships when the purpose is complete.
♦   As we say goodbye to a friendship, another more ideal one arrives for both of us. When we move on, we allow the new friendship to come in.

EXERCISE: How to Let Go of a Friendship

When you let go of a friend, you can do so gently over a period of time and with compassion. It starts with a conscious decision to move on, but it's not necessary to be blunt, although it's okay if you want to be! When you realize this is something you need to do, you will find yourself gradually withdrawing. You will see them less and less, until the amount of contact is appropriate for both of you.

EXERCISE: Attracting Inspirational Friendships

Firstly, decide that you are open to new friendships, that you are entitled to inspiring friendships and that you are prepared to let go of current friendships that leave you feeling drained of energy. Later in the book, you will learn how to create goals, and you can include inspirational friendships in your goals.

Even as you plan to move on, be grateful for what your current friendships have provided. As your focus shifts toward an intention to attract inspirational people, you will find these people appearing in your life.

Inspiring people discuss potentials, abundance, creating dreams, being anything you want to be. These people limit their complaints, discuss solutions and improvements to issues in life and are unlikely to gossip. You feel empowered and enthusiastic when you are with them. Imagine yourself with people like this. Expect new opportunities, and be ready to accept invitations you may usually decline. Be flexible and adventurous.

CHAPTER 14

Managing Your Emotions

"When I let go of what I am, I become what I might be."

Lao Tzu

(Chinese Taoist philosopher and founder of Taoism, 600–531 BC)

*M*ake it a goal to be as calm and peaceful as possible most of the time, and eventually all of the time. Until people master themselves, they usually have something that sets off limited emotions – triggers for anger, frustration, depression, and so on. Limited emotions can make people ill and cause them to lose access to their wisdom and common sense. Someone who is quick to anger will struggle to stay on track to achieve their dream. Limited emotions drag us down; we feel sluggish and unworthy.

By contrast, emotions that induce love, joy and happiness have an invigorating effect on the body. It is possible to be tranquil and composed most, if not all, of the time. Start by loving and accepting yourself, no matter how you behave. Anything you want, you can have.

"If you are patient in one moment of anger, you will escape a hundred days of sorrow."

Chinese Proverb

Going Round in Circles

Through our experiences on Earth, most of us develop unwanted or limited emotions and beliefs, and these adversely affect our lives.[3]

We get stuck in these emotions, and are prevented from participating in new opportunities and discovering more. When we constantly have knee-jerk reactions to the same situations, we go round in circles – we need to free the emotion using the *Release Emotion Technique* (see Appendix A). Otherwise, this blocks our growth.

Release the Emotion in the Moment

> *"Difficult times always create opportunities for you to experience more love in your life."*
>
> Barbara De Angelis
> (American researcher on relationships and personal growth)

Challenges assist you in finding unwanted habitual emotions. These emotions usually exhibit as painful feelings, and we all know them: jealousy, guilt, envy, bitterness, arrogance, revenge, anger, anxiety, lack, grief, sadness, self-pity. When you feel one emotion, the others join in. They are directly linked to a survival mentality, and to fear. They are unpleasant, and they sabotage your dreams. When something triggers an emotion, it is ready for release. Choose to release it. This is part of your evolution.

The energy from these emotions can be freed when you intentionally choose to release them.[9] By releasing unwanted emotions and therefore fear, you cease reacting impulsively and irrationally to challenging situations. When you're behaving impulsively and irrationally, you attract more low-level frequencies. You shift to a higher frequency when you are able to view situations calmly and objectively.

Many therapies advise us to find the source of the emotion and then deal with it. This can be useful, but it can take a long time in therapy to find the source of every emotion in every circumstance. Many of these methods require you to relive the experiences, which can be distressing, as it puts you back in your past. The *Release Emotion Technique* (see Appendix A) ensures that you manage and release an emotion in the moment when it happens, without the need to label it or know where it comes from. If an emotion bothers you, set it free.

"A pessimist sees the difficulty in every opportunity; an optimist sees the opportunity in every difficulty."
Winston Churchill
(U.K. Prime Minister 1940–1945 and 1951–1955
who was noted for his speeches, 1874–1965)

A Little Effort Produces a Rich Return

Because of your focus, these emotions may even seem to appear more often. Part of the journey is to love and accept yourself through this process, and to release the emotions along the way. By releasing the emotion, you can resolve several issues at once because of the ripple effect: when you heal one part of yourself, you positively influence other parts.

Self-esteem and harmony increase in your life as you clear up unwanted emotions, and you then gain freedom, awareness, greater health and motivation to take action towards your goals.

Summary of

"Managing Your Emotions"

- Create an intention to be calm and peaceful most of the time.
- Limiting emotions and beliefs prevent us from discovering new ideas and greater ways of living, and block our growth.
- Challenges trigger unwanted habitual emotions.
- When you feel one emotion, you feel them all in a ripple effect.
- Releasing unwanted emotions lifts your frequency.
- By releasing one emotion you positively influence other parts of yourself.
- Love and accept yourself through the process.

EXERCISE: How to Find and Manage

Unwanted Emotion

One by one:
1.   Pick a situation that causes you to feel stressed.

2. Write the situation down, and think of ways you can be aware of the emotion as it happens. For example, driving to work may be an irrational emotional experience for you, but because it has become such a habit, you are unaware of the effects on your body.
3. Be ready in the moment, and have the intention to use the *Release Emotion Technique* (see Appendix A).

How to stay composed:
1. Only take on as much as you can. Actively manage your workload, and act to avoid certain situations if they invoke emotions you can't yet handle. Use challenges to learn about yourself, but don't look for trouble. The more you are able to stay calm, the better you will handle any challenges you do encounter.
2. If you must face a tough situation, consider ways you can make it easier for yourself. Point out to yourself the benefits of staying calm, and pretend you have always been composed in this situation. Imagine yourself breezing through it.
3. Use challenges as a chance to grow. Intention and motivation are the keys. If you want to grow, you will learn from the situation; if self-pity is still attractive, you won't. This is another reason to build awareness. When you are aware, you can recognize a challenging situation before it arrives. You can encourage yourself to be strong and composed, and tell yourself it is an opportunity to learn.
4. Try to avoid deciding if something is 'good' or 'bad', and simply let things 'be'. If you are in traffic and someone drives badly or cuts you off, let it be. Getting irate only hurts you; the person is on their way and you're still feeling angry. What does it really matter, anyway? If someone is having a bad day and is rude to you, let them be. There is no need for their bad day to affect your blissful one. Step back and observe how calm you are, and what a wonderful day it is. Count your blessings. With practice and intention, you can achieve this.

5. Once you love yourself enough, you will tend to be in a calm and peaceful state of mind most of the time. The ideal outcome is to get to a place where very little ruffles you. Then, it will be easy to spot an unwanted emotion. Be kind to yourself.

CHAPTER 15

Releasing the Fear of Change

"You never find yourself until you face the truth."

Pearl Bailey

(American singer and actress, 1918–1990)

Facing change is one of the biggest fears people encounter. You need flexibility and adaptability – the ability to change, to build your dream life. If we're open and honest, we can all recognize fear in ourselves. Fear is about what could happen, not about what is happening. We create our own fear, and it is just an illusion. Fear may cause people to behave irrationally, arrogantly or aggressively.

"Courage is the power to let go of the familiar."

Raymond Lindquist

(Author, Notes for Living)

Moving On From the Status Quo

No matter how tantalizing the potential outcome, many people fear change in their lives because the body fears the unknown and it fears losing its identity. The wanted or unwanted aspects of our identity are familiar, like a comfortable pair of shoes. We find comfort in the boundaries of our old strengths and weaknesses.

The body may go on high alert for several reasons – when we attempt to think differently, when we have a decision to make or when contemplating an unresolved part of our life. The body cannot ascertain the full consequence of the change and how the change will affect its ability to survive, and it fears its inability to cope in a new situation. It would rather stay as it is, even if it is suffering or unhappy.

"Action conquers fear."

Peter Nivio Zarlenga
(Author, The Orator)

Just Do It

The body can procrastinate by popping up endless questions to delay action so as to stay 'safe'. People may feel confusion as to which path to take, so they procrastinate. Procrastination is borne out of the fear of change, yet any action, even some preliminary research, takes you closer to the real answer. Any action is progress, even if it isn't in the best direction. There is no such thing as a 'wrong' action, no such thing as a 'mistake'. Doing nothing achieves nothing. Each action takes you closer to your goal. Action helps you feel more in control, and gets the energy moving. Action is always preferable to endless procrastination.

Knowledge Gives You Confidence

Despite fear, most people still find themselves drawn to new information, to the unknown, to new potentials, knowing intuitively that there is something out there that will bring more happiness and fulfilment. The more knowledge you gain, the easier it is for you to change. You'll think differently, you're more open, and the fear of change lifts.

New knowledge is exciting and inspiring, and our soul thrives on change. Understanding the reasons for fear gives you courage to look within, to start mastering yourself and allow yourself to find ways to follow your dreams. You are then replacing the fear with fresh, uplifting knowledge and ideas. At the very least, you will experience a tentative excitement as to the possibilities. It is difficult for fear to remain in this environment, especially when you are keen to try out new information and ideas.

Every Step Brings You More Freedom

Take at least a small step toward change. No matter how small the step is, it's still a step. By changing, you are also taking the control from the body. Fear diminishes as you start to experience the unknown and your new identity.

You experience a sense of victory through being brave enough to take action, and you suddenly have freedom to fulfil your potentials. Freedom is a powerful feeling. You feel lighter, filled with love, and you embrace others more. You achieve more of your goals and you are more fun to be around. That's got to be good. It allows more of your true and wonderful self to shine through.

Summary of

"Releasing the Fear of Change"

♦ Fear is about what could happen, not what is happening.
♦ The more knowledge you have, the less you fear change.
♦ The body fears change because it is afraid it won't cope in the new situation. The new situation is an unknown to the body.
♦ Even when we want to make changes, we can find ourselves procrastinating, which is another form of fear. Any action is always better than no action.
♦ It is difficult for fear to remain in an environment of uplifting knowledge and ideas.
♦ Make your first step as small as you want to. Each step allows the body the opportunity to experience the unknown, and yet still feel safe.

EXERCISE: How to Release Fear

1. Make a list of any limiting fearful thoughts and beliefs you might have.
2. Contemplate what it is that prevents you from considering new ideas or making changes.

3. Carry a small notebook with you for a week, and in one column, make a note of your thoughts when you notice concern, anxiety, fear, procrastination or limiting beliefs. In an adjoining column, write alternative inspirational, uplifting statements.

4. To deal with unwanted thoughts, follow the instructions in the exercise 'How to Consciously Choose Thoughts' in Chapter 3 *Whatever You Think Is True*.

5. When you notice a fear, stop for thirty seconds and apply the *Release Emotion Technique* (See Appendix A).

Once again, if you have a motivation, an intention to clear these thoughts from your mind, you will do so. We only need to put in a small amount of effort and focus. Keep going until you achieve freedom – do whatever it takes.

CHAPTER 16
Gratitude

"The invariable mark of wisdom is to see the miraculous in the common."

Ralph Waldo Emerson
(American poet, lecturer and essayist, 1803–1882)

*A*cknowledging your blessings and achievements instantly adds satisfaction to your life. We keep wishing for more, and yet neglect to notice the gifts we already have. Life is about enjoying the journey, so add to your happiness by catching those gifts along the way. Gratitude is underestimated and usually neglected. Unless you are aware of and appreciate your current blessings, you won't value your dreams when they arrive. In fact, you may not even detect their arrival. There is something worth appreciating in every aspect of your life: your relationships, finances, health, job, and so on. It is empowering to focus on what you already have, and doing so attracts more good fortune.

"We can only be said to be alive in those moments when our hearts are conscious of our treasures."

Thornton Wilder
(American playwright and novelist, 1897–1975)

The Beauty Is in the Detail

Involve yourself in the simplest details, such as the fact you can breathe, indeed that you can breathe by yourself, that you can walk, and so on. Perhaps ponder as well the marvel of being alive. Merely saying half-heartedly, 'I am grateful for my health' (yawn) simply won't do it. Come from the heart and become so present with every nuance of your health that you jolt yourself into realizing, 'Hey, I am rather fortunate.' Likewise, as you reflect on your day, you will find plenty of hidden good fortune, even in challenges you may have had. Embrace your surroundings by getting into the beauty of nature. Again, the detail draws you into being captivated by its magnificence. Every thought you have is training your brain toward awareness.

We often only appreciate aspects of our life once they are gone. A friend of mine was in a major car accident several years ago. She broke her neck, and was saved through surgery. We were all thrilled when she recovered, however once she was well again, she discovered that she had no sense of smell or taste. My friend is a very happy, positive person and initially she got on with life, feeling happy to be alive, that she could walk, and so on. Over time though, her lack of ability to taste became a huge frustration for her. Her situation shows how we take the simplest things for granted. The ability to taste is so out of our awareness it seems almost trivial, yet if it is removed, it drastically affects our lives.

Gratitude Constantly Adds to Your Life

Sometimes people choose resistance over gratitude. They obsess over their current circumstances, and the last thing they want to do is accept things the way they are. It was Carl Jung who said, 'What you resist persists', so if you are resisting or detesting your current life, it means you are constantly thinking about what is 'wrong' with it, so you keep attracting more 'wrong'.

By contrast, gratitude snowballs through your life, pulling in more of what you want in all areas. Gratitude grows your objectivity, therefore you are automatically more patient, compassionate, understanding and accepting of yourself and others. These qualities in turn attract a greater life. When you are aware, life flows more freely – the ideal circumstances and the ideal people appear out of the blue to help you to your goal, and you notice them. This boosts your confidence. Your daily life becomes fulfilling and easier with all the support you are receiving. By being grateful for coincidences and rewards, you keep attracting more help to take you toward your goal.

Gratitude Has No Boundaries

It may merely be a change of attitude that enables you to view your life or a situation differently. Gratitude means you accept and love yourself for who you are and what you have, and it's liberating. You'll realize there are infinite things for which to be grateful. Every moment is special. Gratitude has no boundaries, and provides a magical foundation from which to launch your dream life.

Giving Thanks to Others

Express your appreciation to others. Even if you are paying for a service, appreciation still plays a part. Be thankful you attracted a person who loves their job and does it well. Show them respect, and express your appreciation for their friendliness, commitment, professionalism, and so on. They will be inspired, and therefore motivated to give everyone even greater service. In addition, remember to appreciate those closest to you. We tend to make a note of thanking those outside our family, perhaps because we want to impress them, whereas we already feel safely loved by our family. When you express appreciation to someone close, especially for the inconspicuous aspects of your relationship, you deepen and reaffirm your bond.

When the Going Gets Tough, use Gratitude

Gratitude is a major asset during challenging times. Concerns are alleviated, and it also brings you into the present, into the 'now'. When you stay present, it means you are alert to seizing each moment and living life to the full. The only moment that matters is now. If you have to, pretend you are having a fabulous time. Your brain believes everything you think.

Harmony Is Hypnotic, Remain Aware

When you are constantly grateful, you are less likely to become complacent. If you are experiencing challenges, you are active and busy overcoming them. Harmony, on the other hand, can cause a trance-like state, breeding complacency, which in turn creates challenges. Complacency means you become idle, are barely aware, and assume everything will continue as it is – except it doesn't.

> *"Even if you're on the right track, you'll get run over if you just sit there."*
>
> Will Rogers
> (US humorist and showman, 1879–1935)

Life is constantly changing, whether you want it to or not. Couples who cease focusing on their marriage fall into complacency or become engrossed in other parts of their lives, and then take their partner for granted. This is the reason they are shocked when their partner leaves. Always endeavour to acknowledge what you have and treasure it – in all areas of your life. This raises your awareness, and you consequently pay more attention and maintain your focus on what is important. The greater the value you put on your current life, the happier you'll be and the more incentive you'll have to keep it interesting, thereby continuing to attract an even greater life.

> *"If a fellow isn't thankful for what he's got, he isn't likely to be thankful for what he's going to get."*
>
> Frank A Clark

Acknowledge Your Achievements

As for your achievements, they will also get overlooked if you are not in the habit of appreciating your life. If you are continually waiting for results and getting frustrated, develop your ability to detect changes as they occur. They are definitely there, sometimes outside of you, sometimes within you – it may simply be an attitude change. It's worth revealing these, as you can immediately start celebrating the fruits of your efforts. You'll probably be quite impressed by what you've achieved.

Relish what you already have. Gratitude is a springboard toward your dream life.

Summary of "Gratitude"

+ It is important to notice and appreciate current blessings, otherwise you'll overlook your dreams when they arrive.
+ Appreciating your life today immediately adds to your life. It empowers you and attracts more good fortune.
+ Learn to view and appreciate life from different perspectives.
+ Appreciate the subtle aspects of your life as well as the more obvious aspects.
+ Gratitude helps you become more patient, compassionate, understanding and accepting.
+ Be sure to notice the people and circumstances that appear to help you toward your goal, as this motivates you and keeps you aware that you are continually attracting more help to take you toward your goal.
+ Gratitude means you accept and love yourself. The greater your love for yourself the greater your life.
+ There are an infinite number of things for which to be grateful.
+ Thank others for their service, even if you are paying them. Remember to appreciate those closest to you for the little things they do.
+ Gratitude is a major asset during challenging times, because you gain perspective when you draw your attention toward appreciating what you have.
+ When you are grateful, you are less likely to become complacent about your life.

◆   Develop your ability to detect changes as they occur. When the results arrive along the way, you can immediately celebrate your achievements.

EXERCISE: How to be Grateful

Make a List:

1. As a one-off exercise, find time by yourself and focus on everything in your life you can be grateful for. Include the smallest details, such as being able to see, hear, breathe, having a warm bed at night, food to eat, water to drink. Remember to include having the ability to participate in life, to experience nature, having love in your life, your attitudes, friends, family, health, money, your clothes, furniture, your car, the knowledge you have, your future and the wisdom you have gained. Even include things like your local shopping center, where you can easily buy food, clothing and so on. The list is infinite. Everyone has different blessings in their life. Your role is to notice them and appreciate them.

2. You will surprise yourself at what comes to mind when you do this exercise. It seems the longer the list, the more you find to add to it.

Make It a Part of Your Day:

1. If you are new to gratitude, try to arrange a routine so that you can remember to do it regularly and to notice the specifics from each day.

2. You may choose to do it as you fall asleep at night, as you wake up, or as you shower. It is a good idea to choose a time when your mind can wander freely, yet remain focused on finding those things for which to be grateful.

3. You can also sit quietly and write everything in a special journal.

EXERCISE: How to Celebrate Your Achievements

1. List everything you have ever achieved but haven't yet recognized. Include even the smallest aspects of your life. You'll be amazed.
2. List any challenges you have overcome. For each one, congratulate yourself on your courage and tenacity, and notice what you gained.

CHAPTER 17

Abundance

"Not what we have but what we enjoy, constitutes our abundance."

Epicurus
(Greek philosopher, 341–270 BC)

Whatever you focus on, you experience.[3] The more you notice abundance, the more you have it. The more generous you are, the more generous others are to you. The more grateful you are, the more you have. Abundance is everywhere you look – you merely need the willingness to notice it. You'll always have everything you need to follow your soul's desires.

"There are people who have money and people who are rich."

Coco Chanel
(French fashion designer, 1883–1971)

Financial Wealth Isn't Necessarily Abundance

If a wealthy person lacks purpose or fulfilment, the money is disregarded. Wealthy people may become apathetic, bored and depressed or turn to drugs and alcohol if they have empty, meaningless lives.

The origin of the word abundance is 'to overflow'. True abundance means we have plenty of whatever makes us happy, and we have a generous heart – we are fulfilled, for we have more than we need.

One person may be poor, yet fulfilled, happy and generous, while another may be rich, yet sad and frugal. To develop true abundance, you need purpose to your life. You develop purpose when you realize you are here to learn to love yourself, to master being in a body, to seek new experiences to get what you want and to evolve to greater wisdom.[3]

There Is Plenty for Everyone

Much of the world views life from the position of scarcity. Career paths, money and relationships are often perceived as being in short supply or restricted. Wrong. You can always have what you want without others missing out. If you want what others have, then there is enough for you too, although always be sure that the dream is your dream, not someone else's.

"We must become the change we want to see."
Mahatma Gandhi
(Political and spiritual Leader of India and the Indian Independence Movement, 1869–1948)

What Is Behind the Money

Many people think being wealthy is to be happy, but firstly we need balance in our lives. Money or material items can never make you happy if you have an empty life or unresolved emotional issues such as insecurity, inferiority, jealously, bitterness, and so on. When working with wealth, it is useful to work on several areas of your life at one time.

Whatever you feel money provides you – freedom, happiness, equality, peace, security – is the quality you need to develop in order to become more magnetic to money. The richest person in the world is still likely to feel insecure unless they have developed aspects such as confidence and trust. This empowers them, and they can then feel secure. Otherwise, more money will cause even greater insecurity if they are concerned about losing it.

The Power of an Attitude of Abundance

Paul needed to create a voluntary committee. He had heard that it was going to be a tough job to find people, so he decided to operate from an attitude of abundance imagining that he always had more than enough willing committee members. When he approached people, he always checked whether they were keen to join, because he felt there was no purpose in having people who didn't want to be there. Paul believed he would always easily find the ideal person for the job, and this is exactly what happened. He continued to form new committees year after year, effortlessly. When some people didn't want to attend meetings, he told them the meetings were part of the fun, but that it was fine if they couldn't make them, and perhaps they could attend as many as possible. By being flexible in this way, he found that most meetings had record attendances.

Paul also assured people that if they didn't like the job, they could leave at any time. There is no sense in someone continuing in a voluntary position if it's unsuitable for them, so Paul let go of the fear that they might leave. People are more likely to join and stay when they have freedom to leave. A few people did leave, but at least Paul knew that the people who stayed wanted to be there. Our attitude can bring out the best in people.

Small business owners find it especially helpful to adopt an attitude of abundance. They often have close relationships with their clients, such that after several years the client finds it difficult to leave. None of us enjoys obligation, and this relationship is similar to friendships that are past their use-by date. Even though it's hard to let go of a client, by having an attitude of abundance, the small business owner ensures a steady supply of wonderful new clients. Ironically, the existing clients are more likely to stay. As the small business owner allows freedom of choice for their clients, so they provide it for themselves. Abundance always allows freedom and a greater result.

Dave was fairly new to a large organization, and he and a colleague in his team were in line for promotion. Both had an attitude of abundance, and neither used under-handed techniques to gain favour.

Dave understood the importance of focusing on his dream, and set the scene for having such a position. He chose to let go of how it would happen. They both continued doing their jobs as usual. Soon afterward, Dave's colleague announced that he had found a job with another organization. It was that simple. Dave received the promotion, and saw it confirmed once again that we can all achieve results that suit everyone without orchestrating the details ourselves.

Decide to Have Enough for Whatever You Want

If you only had a $20 note in your purse, you might think you have to work to a budget of $20, and from one perspective you're correct, as that is the reality you have created, and whatever we think is true for us.

To create abundance, we need to change our attitude and our thoughts. Instead of telling ourselves we only have a certain amount till the end of the week, we tell ourselves we always have more than enough for whatever we need or want at any time. The first option limits us and focuses on lack, while the second focuses on abundance and freedom without concern for how we achieve it.

Again in regard to balance, it is crucial to understand that although many people focus on just getting by, other people either spend all their money irrationally, or use credit to spend money they don't have. Generally, it is an attitude of scarcity that causes this behavior. They believe they don't have enough money, but spend it anyway. They are usually endeavouring to find prestige, happiness and love through the items they purchase, but the moment of joy is fleeting. This is an addiction similar to overeating, drugs or alcohol. It's a recipe for financial disaster, and another way people create challenges for themselves.

Your Fulfilment Grants You True Abundance

Determine what it is about money that helps you, and set about satisfying those needs in other ways. It is different for each individual, and it is your responsibility to find what makes you happy. Once you have achieved greater fulfilment in yourself, you naturally attract everything you want as a natural flow-on effect.

Life is considerably simpler and easier with an abundance attitude. When your attitude is abundance, you change your mind from 'That's impossible' to 'I can do anything'.

Summary of
"Abundance"

♦ Financial wealth doesn't mean abundance. True abundance means we have plenty of whatever makes us truly happy, and we have a generous heart – we are fulfilled, we have more than we need.

♦ You can always have what you want, and there will also be enough for others.

♦ By being grateful for what you have, you immediately have more abundance.

♦ When seeking abundance, discover what it is about having abundance that will satisfy you. This is the quality you need to work on, and you will attract abundance as a result. The money itself will not bring satisfaction. We need to know how money helps us.

♦ An attitude of abundance can also help you achieve your dreams in the workplace.

♦ Some people just get by each day, while others behave irrationally and overspend. Both operate from a position of lack. Neither feels worthwhile, nor creates long-term fulfilment.

♦ The key to creating happiness and getting what you want is following your own interests. The more fulfilled you are, the more abundance you attract.

EXERCISE: How to Bring Abundance into
Your Awareness

1. Being aware of abundance takes intention and training. Firstly, you need to become aware of when you limit yourself or when you observe limitation anywhere in your

world, such as becoming overly sensitive to the price of grocery items, or even being pessimistic when looking for a parking space at the mall on a busy Saturday. You become more restricted with every limiting thought you have. If you can catch these thoughts, you have the opportunity to intervene and convince yourself to choose abundance – to have available to you anything you want. The brain works so fast that this can all be done in a split second. As you continually do this, your mind naturally starts to notice limiting thoughts, gets faster at spotting them, and can immediately replace them with abundance.

2. How does having more money assist you? What deeper part of you will be satisfied when you have more money? Analyze how you feel when you have access to a large amount of cash, when you buy a new item of clothing, an item for the house or when you buy a new car. There is always an immediate strong reaction, which somehow helps you. Your goal is to discover what that benefit is. Ask yourself how your life or feelings change once you have this item, or when you have more money. Understanding this will help you provide these advantages without the need for money. You can change your attitude to move away from needing another person or a force such as money in your life to make you happy. You have the power to independently decide and control your life. Then money finds you anyway.

3. Make use of affirmations to remind you of your abundance. Affirmations keep you present and focused on your dream. Affirmations are described in detail at the end of the book in Section 6 *The Gift of Every New Day*. Place obvious 'abundance' reminders around your house. Create affirmations such as:

- I have everything I want and need.
- I get what I want.
- Happiness is my life.
- I am grateful for the abundance in my life now.
- I am grateful for my healthy body.
- I am fulfilled in every corner of my being.
- Every day I recognize the abundance in my life.
- I create anything I want.

- I love and trust myself.
- Every day I become more magnetic to money.
- Good things come to me easily.
- I easily magnetize money.
- I create abundance through loving myself.
4. Place notes such as these or pictures of what abundance means to you in the bedroom, bathroom, office and car. These keep you on track throughout the day. Flood your day with them, and you will become more aware of abundance. Change them regularly, so they are fresh and noticeable.

CHAPTER 18

Happy Mind, Healthy Body

"What we think we become."

Buddha

*H*ealth is often attributed to good luck or bad luck, but fortunately, *you* decide your own health. Admittedly, most people are not at the required level to heal the more complicated diseases without help or intervention, but this varies from person to person. It is vital that you understand that you have the power to heal yourself of anything.[3] The more you accept that you can get anything you want, the greater this power.

There are numerous reasons people don't heal themselves – in the case of a victim mentality, the disease 'benefits' them in some way, and deep down they don't want to change, or it may be due to lack of knowledge and doubts about their ability to do so. You build belief in healing yourself by learning more about using your brain to heal, and by healing yourself whenever you can. You'll find yourself getting healthier every day, and increasingly able to heal yourself in greater ways. When you do, you assist those around you by helping them to build belief in their own ability to heal.

Your Body Is Proof of What You Are Thinking

"Warning: Humor may be hazardous to your illness."

Ellie Katz Ph.D RN

When you are happy and fulfilled, it shows in your body. If you are distressed, so is your body. If you live in fear of a threatening disease, that is your focus, and you attract it.

What you say reflects your thoughts, of course, so when it comes to your health, it is essential to be mindful of your speech. Notice how much discussion is invoked by the latest cold or flu virus. People avidly discuss how bad they are feeling, or who had the worst experience. Each person seems to have a more dreadful picture to paint. As you can probably guess, anyone who *competes* for the 'worst' ill health attracts more ill health. Tune in to what people are saying – and be ready to leap out of the way.

Empower Your Mind

Sometimes doctors don't have the answer to a problem, but they may not tell you this. Most of them rely on prescribing drugs, and haven't explored the powers of the mind in healing. Even if they did, they would probably underestimate your self-healing abilities, because it isn't necessarily in their interest to explore self-healing.

There are stories of cases where the doctor said the patient had two months to live, and two months later the patient died. Was the doctor accurate in the prediction, or did the patient believe they would die in that time-frame? Both are possible, but it's more likely the patient kept to the 'deadline'. Thoughts of health and thoughts of death are equally powerful – you merely choose which one you want.

A person's attitude determines whether an ailment requires a doctor's intervention. All diseases can be healed through a change of attitude, a new way of thinking, a change of lifestyle or via assistance from 'alternative medicine' – often without drugs or surgery.

"Every human being is the author of his own health or disease."

Buddha

Many aches, pains and illnesses appear as a result of unhappiness and dissatisfaction, i.e. unhelpful emotions or limiting beliefs. Assess the area of the body where the disorder is manifesting. This may give you clues as to what created the

143

illness.[3] Louise Hay's book *You Can Heal Your Life* has helped me many times. It has a list of illnesses, their probable causes and an affirmation to heal your issue.

Search through all areas of your life: relationships, jobs, thoughts, beliefs, attitudes and frustrations. Perhaps you are bored, and need more purpose. Alternatively, you may be too busy, or may enjoy the attention of ill health. By forming sentences in your brain that indicate with genuine intent that you want an answer to your issue, the ideas and opportunities will start arriving. The easiest and fastest way to radiant health is to keep learning about yourself, make new discoveries, create new experiences aligned with your soul, and constantly choose thoughts of health and possibility.

The more fulfilled you are, the healthier you are. Look after your body – sleep well, eat well, drink sufficient water and do gentle exercise. However, these only work to create health when your thoughts are aligned with health and happiness, and when you understand that you will have boundless energy and vitality.

Health is Another Journey of Discovery

Challenges always relate to a journey of discovery. In regard to acquiring radiant health, it is a path that can take you on a journey toward health as well as empowering knowledge. As always, keep searching until your health is ideal. Never give up. Your body has the capacity for absolute radiant health.

> *"There is nothing in a caterpillar that tells you it's going to be a butterfly."*
> Richard Buckminster Fuller
> (American architect, author, designer, futurist, inventor and visionary, 1895–1983)

Anything Is Possible – Even Healing Yourself

For some, the illness may be genetic, but contrary to popular opinion, these illnesses can also be healed through our thoughts. The label 'genetic' can seem huge and insurmountable, but do yourself a favour and imagine the disease as small and insignificant, but *totally curable*. There is nothing to lose and everything to gain. Give your fabulous brain every opportunity to heal you.

You already have the best answer in you, but keep in mind that new solutions are continually becoming available – never give up the search. Consider the emergence of neuroplasticity; the discovery that the brain can change itself. This impressive discovery reignited the hopes of millions of people affected by cerebral palsy, learning disabilities, dyslexia, schizophrenia and many other neurological issues; the list goes on. One of the best aspects is that many of the radical improvements are achieved through the mind, eliminating the need for operations or medication.

Additionally, neuroplasticity has demonstrated our ability to turn genes on and off through our thinking. The significance of this is huge. It means that simply by using powerful thoughts, we can keep a genetic illness at bay or even access different DNA to heal completely. We are no longer forced to live with the DNA with which we were born.[6,7] Again, always be persistent in your mission to discover your answer.

Constantly champion your own cause by staying alert for new discoveries. If there is a scientific breakthrough for an illness or disability, you can hardly expect your doctor to make contact and inform you of the development. Take responsibility for your health.

"You need to make a commitment, and once you make it, then life will give you some answers."

Les Brown
(American author, entrepreneur and motivational speaker)

Commitment Is All You Need to Achieve Health

While healing through your own endeavours sounds simple, it does require motivation and consistent mental effort to make changes. The mind–body connection is obviously a huge subject, and the preceding section has only been a very basic explanation, however the aim here is to call your attention to your potentials. We only use a very small portion of our brain, while the rest of it sits unused, ready and waiting for us to access our unlimited potential.[3]

Cultivate Your Acceptance, Educate Yourself

For someone with an illness, this may sound too idealistic or simplistic, therefore it is important to continue to learn to grow your acceptance levels. Further reading is highly recommended, as it unlocks even more of your magnificent potentials. Appendix B lists several books that delve deeper into this science. Reading inspirational real-life stories about self-healing increases your acceptance of this possibility. All these potentials are available to you, and learning more about your brain and body captivates your imagination and paves the way for you to access your potentials. Even choosing one new enlightening thought drives you toward greater health.

Healing Yourself Through Harmonious Healthcare

Consider natural solutions where possible. Society has moved from relying on natural answers to being conditioned to rely exclusively on chemical medicine. It's now time to regain a sense of balance and relinquish our dependence on doctors for minor health issues such as colds and flu. Let's move on from needing reassurance that we are healthy. The body is a powerful organism that is more naturally aligned with health than disease. It might be hard to believe in our society, but yes, given the chance, the body will always move toward a higher order of health, rather than down to disease.

Most of us have been persuaded that something chemically manufactured is greater than natural therapy. We generally love instant results, and so we choose chemical drugs. It's long been known that they can be miraculous, and have saved the lives of millions, but many drugs have an adverse effect on the body, and while the symptom may be cured temporarily, the cause remains. It is comforting that drugs are there as an option, but it is always preferable to heal naturally. Natural remedies create greater long-term benefits.

We are now seeing a swing toward natural therapy, and a combination of both natural therapy and chemical drugs can work wonders. It is worth contemplating how natural therapies could ever have come to be known as 'alternative' therapies.

There are many natural therapies available to support you during recovery from colds and flu, along with rest and plenty of fluid. These give the body the opportunity to heal itself and boost its immune system. By doing this a few times, you gain belief and confidence in your ability to heal minor ailments without medical intervention. This presses you forward to the ultimate achievement of radiant health every day.

If you give alternative medicine a go, keep in mind that the power of your thoughts plays a part in the result. If you are reluctantly trying it and feeling sceptical, you are limiting your outcome. You get what you expect. Give the medicine the best chance by expecting a major breakthrough in your health. Focus on getting what you want.

"Take care of your body. It's the only place you have to live."
Jim Rohn
(American motivational speaker and author, b. 1930)

Wisdom Is Your Reward for Your Effort

Regardless of the outcome, when you intentionally use thoughts to heal yourself, you store your experience and consequent understanding as wisdom – which you keep eternally.[3] Even if initially it seems that your health is deteriorating, this is movement; something is happening. In all areas of life, including health, things often seem to get worse before they get better. This can be put down to the reorganization of the brain that is taking place. Stick with it, continue to learn and keep using thoughts to create your ideal situation.

Health = Power for You

Health is a worthy focus. The healthier you are, the more your body will humbly serve you on your journey of discovery. You will be more powerful, and have more energy to make powerful choices. It's worth considering.

You Choose the Best Option for You

Note that it is important to always keep your inner compass handy. You should be the judge of what is required for you to achieve radiant health. These suggestions are designed to expand your options, highlight the natural healing abilities of the body and enable you to use your brain to confidently steer you towards strength and vitality every day. Only use these ideas if they resonate with you, and if the timing is right. The ultimate decision and responsibility is always yours.

Conscious Thought Takes You Higher

As you practice being conscious of your thoughts, you will find that you naturally gravitate to higher thoughts. You will launch yourself to new heights of fulfilment and empowerment, and ensure that your body is stronger than it has ever been before.

Summary of

"Happy Mind, Healthy Body"

♦ You have the power to heal yourself of anything.
♦ Your health is a reflection of your thoughts.
♦ The more happy and fulfilled you are, the healthier you will be.
♦ Most illnesses appear as a result of unhappy, limited thoughts and when you are unable to do what you want.
♦ The more we heal ourselves, the more we believe we can heal anything.
♦ Be mindful of your words when discussing your health with others.
♦ Keep searching for answers until you are satisfied with your health.
♦ Continue learning about health and healing to grow your acceptance that anything is possible.
♦ Consider using natural therapies over chemical medicine.
♦ The healthier you are, the more powerful you are, and the greater your achievements.
♦ Ultimately, your health is your decision, and you should feel comfortable in your approach.

EXERCISE: How to Use Your Brain to Achieve Health

1. Start with an open mind. Ask yourself whether you are prepared to consider being healthy.
2. Recognize that this is a journey to learn that this is possible, a journey to learn how to do it and a journey to put it into practice. Resist the need for instant results.
3. Be prepared to put in the required mental effort to learn what you currently do to create your health. In addition, decide to learn how your brain and body works and acknowledge that your thinking needs to be adjusted in order to create your ideal health.
4. Remind yourself of what you want every day with affirmations placed around your home, in your car, and so on. Then create your dream using the exercise in Chapter 19 *Creating Your Dreams*. As you continue reading you'll find several exercises in the coming chapters that assist you in becoming more aware of your thoughts.
5. Grow further by reading other books on this subject. Every book explains the concept slightly differently, but as always, we only benefit when we take the information and actually use it in our daily lives.

EXERCISE: How to Maintain or Create a Healthy Body

1. Become aware of your opinions about health and your beliefs about the strength of your own body. Notice the words you use regarding health. Do you believe you 'catch' colds without choice?
2. When friends are complaining about their health, notice whether or not you join in to discuss your health issues. It's only too easy to find ourselves sharing issues, as it helps us feel accepted and included. Doing this puts your health in jeopardy. All conversations create your reality. What you say becomes

what you experience. Health is a common topic, and it is easy to get caught up discussing our health as a weakness. Instead, try to avoid these conversations, and change the subject at the first opportunity. Alternatively, think of some health affirmations while your friends are talking. Everyone who resists the temptation to discuss illness and instead focuses on health also helps the community to gain health. If you do get a cold, it will pass quickly if you stay focused on health. Focus on your strong body.

3. The less we talk about illness, the better. Many people expect colds and flu, and as winter approaches they start to prepare for illness. This almost guarantees it. Once winter hits and people start falling ill, the flu topic escalates – it seems impossible to escape, and even more people succumb. It's all in your mind, though – keep your mind sharp and focus on health and vitality. Bear in mind that talking to someone who has a cold has nothing to do with your chances of getting it. You maintain your health according to your attitude.

4. Acknowledge improvements in your health. If previously you got several colds or flu every winter and you have now reduced the number, recognize that as a huge step out of illness and into health. Or perhaps you are now moving through colds more quickly. It all counts.

5. Create affirmations to empower your body to health every day. Ensure the sentences are worded in the present tense. Place them around your home and workplace.
    Here are some examples:

♦   I am powerful and strong.
♦   I am fit and flexible.
♦   I wake up healthy every day.
♦   I go to sleep healthy every day.
♦   I rejuvenate to health in every moment.
♦   All I have ever known is radiant health.
♦   I create radiant health in every moment.

If you are willing to consider these potentials and put in the effort, you are already half way to creating the health you want.

Section 4

Living Your Dreams

*"Go confidently in the direction of your dreams. Live the
life you have imagined."*

Henry David Thoreau
(American author and philosopher,
1817–1862)

We've arrived. Now you create and live your dream life.
Dream big.

There are infinite possibilities for you existing in this
moment in the quantum field. It is now for you to decide which
of those possibilities will be the reality you experience.

> ***Yes, today…and every day…you can just choose
> anything you want!***

But…you must deliberately do the choosing. When you see
someone with abundance, that is what they have *chosen*. If a person's
life is filled with lack, then all they have allowed themselves is a
small portion of their dream, a small aspect of their true potential.

You'll allow in your life as much as you think you are
allowed, or as much as you think is possible. You are responsible
for deciding how abundant or lacking your world is; it all
depends on which potentials you pick.

The following chapters show you how to create your dream
life, and the fastest ways to get it.

CHAPTER 19

Creating Your Dreams

"If you want to live a happy life, tie it to a goal, not to people or things."

Albert Einstein
(German-born theoretical physicist, 1879–1955)

This is where the rubber hits the road. Leap out of your current life and into your dream life. If you want to have your magnificent life, you need to take charge of yourself *now* and *at least* state what it is that you want.

My Experience – Creating My First Dream

Before we get into the technique for creating your dream, here is an example of how this exercise changed my life. I have successfully used this technique in various aspects of my life, but the first time I used it is one of the most memorable. At the time of creating my dream, I had been travelling and working for a few years. I was single, had left my birth country, South Africa, and was living alone in a new country, Australia, far from my family and close friends.

Although I was making friends at work and I was grateful to be living in such a beautiful country, I missed Africa and felt alone without the support of close friends and family.

One day, I was reading a book by Shakti Gawain called Creative Visualization, which describes a technique called your 'Ideal Scene',

This involves describing your ideal situation as if your goal is fully realized. It appeared to be just what I needed, so I purchased a special journal and wrote about my dream day. (Note: I was taking action to create my dream.)

At the time, my dream seemed a huge step up from what I was currently experiencing, and I remember pondering the likelihood of it coming true. Because I was missing my family, I imagined creating my own. I imagined a scene where I had a loving and supportive husband, healthy, happy children and a comfortable house in an established suburb with lots of trees. It was so simple, but I loved creating my dream day. It felt good to take action, and it instantly filled me with hope and possibility.

Once I had completed the story of my dream day, I put the journal aside and rarely looked at the page, because the book had reassured me that even if I never looked at my 'Ideal Scene' again, one day I would stumble upon it in my journal and realize that it was now my reality. This is exactly what happened. Actually, my dream had been fulfilled beyond my expectation. Even now when I re-read that story in my journal, I am filled with amazement at how easy it was to create my life the way I wanted. I didn't know it then, but I was tapping into a potential on the quantum field, and it seemed that in the next breath, I was living it.

The technique I am about to explain is even more powerful than the one I used, because I have added the knowledge and experience I have gathered over the years.

> "We should be taught not to wait for inspiration to start a thing. Action always generates inspiration. Inspiration seldom generates action."
>
> Frank Tibolt
> (Author of A Touch of Greatness, 1897–1989)

You Can Have Anything You Want... but Be Clear

Everything in this world starts with an idea or a dream that someone imagines. The idea or dream *always* comes first. There's no need to wish for a genie; *you* are and have always been the genie that creates your life. Rub the lamp and purposefully create your dream life today. Perhaps you have never thought of what you want (which would be why you haven't got it). It may take some contemplation, which is normal.

The best way to start is by acknowledging that you want to evolve, and you want a magnificent life. Once you have made this a conscious decision, you immediately start to attract what you want, because now you are thinking clearly and intentionally.

It is vital to be clear on what you want – to avoid sending mixed messages into the quantum field. Most people absentmindedly wish for various things in their life, but wishes are 'wishy-washy' in that they are usually half-hearted, and they are varied every day. Very little gets created, and life is monotonous. We need you to be absolutely clear about what you want. This exercise helps you decide what it is you really want. Let go of 'how' it happens. Allow it to unfold in the best way for you.

No Idea What You Want?

If you have no idea what you want, that's okay. Merely take a step back and simply make it your goal, at this stage, to discover what you want; to know your passions in life. Sometimes, we get so bombarded by other people's dreams we struggle to fathom our own. Once you achieve the goal of knowing what you want, you will be uplifted and supremely powerful, because there is something extraordinarily intoxicating in knowing what makes you happy and how to take charge of your own life.

Big or Small...Just Make Sure You are Passionate About It

You can create small goals or big goals. One idea is to create an ideal scene of a major dream and then break it down into smaller parts. You may also choose to focus on one area of your life at a time, or even go for something intangible like more self-love, greater fulfilment, and so on. Smaller goals are excellent. They contribute to your greater life and build confidence, because you see them achieved more quickly. Be sure that you are passionate about the goal, though – it has to be worth imagining.

"The first step binds one to the second."

French Proverb

Create Your Dream Today and Tomorrow Dawns With Your Dream Already In Place

This is a crucial moment. Sometimes, the trickiest part is getting that pen out or sitting down in front of the computer. If you don't have the motivation to create your dream life today, then that day will arrive soon, but remember; you are *choosing* to delay.

If necessary, pacify your body by giving it a reward while you are writing down your dream, or once it is done. Once you are poised for action, the fun begins. Creating this story is the biggest step you can take toward living your dream.

Your Dream Day

1. Start by expressing gratitude for your current life. What you have in your life today was once dreams, too. Getting into the habit of gratitude helps you notice when your goals are being realized. Too often, we want aspects of our life to change, but fail to notice when they do. Noticing them inspires and empowers you to create greater goals. Gratitude also sets the scene for your new dream and creates a frequency for attracting more sensational things into your life.

2. Contemplate any unfinished dreams or tasks you may have on your mind. Either choose to act on them using this exercise, or consciously let them go if they no longer serve a purpose or if they've lost their appeal. There are various reasons why goals or dreams go unrealized. Regardless of whether the dreams were achieved or not, everything you have done has got you to where you are today…and today is all that counts. Sweep your mind clear of old dreams and focus freely on this one.

3. Take a few minutes to go to a special place in your mind (such as described on page 4 of this book) where you feel warm, happy, safe, loved. You might choose an amazing place in nature, a favourite holiday destination – somewhere you love

155

to be. Get comfortable and write this story from your happy place.

4. It's time to consider what you want. Consider an aspect of your life and establish what is and what isn't working. You may find it helps to consider what you *don't* want, and then turn it around to what you *do* want. When it comes to writing, always state things in the positive, i.e. try to avoid words like 'don't' and what you wouldn't like. State what you *do* want.

5. Choose a dream that inspires you. If you are half-hearted about your dream, it is less likely to appear. You need passion and incentive to focus on it and to follow up on opportunities. Otherwise, it's an empty goal.

6. Write down the purpose of this dream. This ensures that you are passionate about this dream, and that it is truly your dream and not someone else's. Determine what you expect the dream to provide for you. In other words, does it provide freedom, joy, adventure, relaxation, abundance, etc.? These are the unconscious intangible benefits you experience. Ascertain what it is about having a new car, a new house, a child or a new job that motivates you to have it. Establish what that satisfaction really means to you. What is the reward?

7. If you are someone who finds visualization a challenge and you work better with feelings and sound, the *intangible benefits* may help you to form your dream, rather than imagining how the dream 'looks'.

8. Contemplate the differences between your dream life and your current situation. How are they different? Include the intangible benefits.

> *"I can't go back to yesterday –because I was a different person then." Alice.*
>
> Lewis Carroll
> (Alice's Adventures in Wonderland, 1832–1898)

9. Imagine beyond your senses. Avoid being logical or sensible; just dream. Avoid conjuring up how you will feel when the dream is realized. You may be asking for fulfilment or freedom in a part of your life, but these will be new sensations for you to experience. This is because you only get the feeling

of the dream once you've lived it.³ Many different people and circumstances may enter your life to create this dream for you, but you have no idea who or what they are, or how you will feel about them. Even if your dream is to create a thriving new business and you have done this previously, avoid using those same feelings to create the new business. You are a different person today to who you were when the previous business was created. Avoid using old feelings to create new feelings. Every day, most people live their lives based on emotions from the past, which is why their lives are the same every day. Boring. However, it is still vital that you feel intense motivation to create your dream. There is a subtle difference between the strong desire of imagining and wanting your dream and feeling the end result.

10. Make your dream about a day in your life as if you are already living it. For example, you wake up one Wednesday morning and everything in your dream has come true. What does this day look like? Everything you want is encapsulated in this day in your life. This is the way you are living your life now. Or, imagine a scene where you are telling someone you just met about the life you live. Describe it to this person as if it is 'now'. Those thoughts immediately start attracting this life to you. Include as many aspects as you want – love, health, family, relationships, career, prosperity, travel, your home, fulfilment, empowerment, inner peace, patience, fun. Avoid sentences that speak of the future, such as 'I will' or 'I would like'. Write the story as if it is 'now' in your life, and you'll find you are imagining it as if it is already here. Use words such as, 'I have', 'I am now', 'I now', 'I am'.

11. Now get on with creating your story and include everything you want – no obligation is allowed. Have fun visualizing. Although this seems crazy, pretend that you already have it all. Step into this person now. Your brain does not know the difference, and will take this as reality. This is your chance to decide your life.

12. Although you want to be clear about your dreams, avoid being too specific in the detail. There is a balance. Allow the quantum field to provide your dream in the best way for

you. By being too specific, you can delay the result, as it halts the natural flow of the quantum field. For example, if you would like a partner, avoid asking for a particular person. The quantum field has all potentials, and already has the ideal person waiting for you; you've just never allowed them in. Your dream may not end up looking exactly like the one you created, but everything you want will be provided.

"Everything you can imagine is real."

Pablo Picasso

(Spanish artist, 1881–1973)

13. As you focus on this magnificent life already being here, forget *how* it will happen. If you find yourself thinking about the 'how', merely refocus on the dream. The quantum field has mysterious ways of creating what you want. Keep your thoughts on your dream, and allow the magic to happen.

14. At the end of your story, include the sentence, 'I create this or something greater, and everyone involved benefits.' (Note: you cannot know what is of 'benefit' to another – the outcome of your dream may not seem to benefit others, but you cannot know what others need in their lives to become greater – merely create the intention to benefit, and allow it.)

15. If you choose to, you can immediately review your story or re-write it to make the dream even bigger. You can have anything you want, so ensure your dream day is as unlimited and as free as possible.

16. Now let's keep this momentum going. Choose dates to review your progress and mark these dates for review in your diary. Make a promise to yourself that you will spend at least five genuine minutes contemplating, whether you think you have achieved anything or not. As you reflect, several achievements *will* appear, and some of them will be intangible. At each review session, record your findings. This is why you need to make sure the dream is wonderful enough for you to be sufficiently motivated to stay focused. Even if you overlook the review sessions, the dates in your diary serve as a reminder for continued focus on your dream. Remember, we

achieve our tasks at work because we have to, so give your own dreams the same level of focus and get what you want.

17. I have deliberately avoided asking you to include specifics, for example if you want to lose weight, how much weight you want to lose, and a date by which you want to have done it. This is often used to make a goal measurable, however setting a date for the future puts the goal into the future. Instead, live as if you are already relishing the fruits of achieving your goal today. Even though you are pretending, your brain takes this on and dives right in to luxuriate in the warm glow of achieving the goal. Go for freedom, not restricting numbers and dates. Passion will always triumph over a deadline. Deadlines work in business, or in the education system, where there are consequences. When the goal is self-appointed, however, under-achieving by a certain date means disappointment as a consequence. You're just plain over dabbling in disappointment, so set yourself up for victory instead.

    Instead of saying

    'I will lose 10kgs by 1 December', say 'I am my ideal weight and I feel fabulous about myself', or 'I am courageous and determined to do whatever it takes to achieve my ideal weight and be happy', or 'Weight falls off me easily until I am my ideal weight.'

    Instead of saying 'By July next year I will be earning an additional $50,000 per year', say 'I am magnificently wealthy with an abundance of money to buy everything I want', or 'I instantly have everything I want', or 'Money flows easily into my life and I'm constantly receiving salary increases.'

18. Of course, if you do find deadlines motivating, feel free to include some. Always feel free to play with whatever works best for you, and allow the quantum field to deliver your best outcome.

19. Your brain loves symbols.[4] A picture is worth a thousand words. As a concluding step to creating your dream life, visualize an image or a symbol that illustrates your dream and draw it onto a card. It can be elaborately decorated, or very simple. Your brain understands what it represents.

Focus on this symbol every night before bed. You could also make a smaller version for your wallet or workstation.

20. Create affirmations about your dream, and plant them around your home and workstation. Keep some in your wallet for inspiration while waiting for an appointment. You are training your brain to naturally think this way. Saturate your life with your dream. Do whatever it takes to stay motivated.

21. As soon as possible, find ways to jump-start your goal. It can be as simple as:

♦ Searching the Internet for ideas
♦ Reading motivational books
♦ Finding books that educate you on your chosen area
♦ Attending courses on the topic
♦ Listening to motivational speakers on CD, iPod, MP3, etc.

22. Finally, understand that the reason you create dreams and goals is to propel you to new experiences and adventures. No matter what the final outcome, you add amazingly to your life in tangible and intangible ways on the path to your dream. Be ready to catch these benefits. In many respects, these are the true gems you gain from setting goals – rather than the final outcome. Feel free to change your dream when you're part of the way toward achieving your goal, as long as you don't change your dream every five minutes!

(Based on the book *Creative Visualization* by Shakti Gawain, specifically the chapter entitled "*Ideal Scene*")

Celebrate...Allow Your Dream to Unfold

This exercise is a simple and easy way to achieve your dreams. Acknowledge your get-up-and-go in creating your dream. Hopefully you enjoyed doing it. Celebrate your new life in a special way: this is an important step you have taken, and opportunities will instantly start opening up for you. There is no need to predict the future. This is already your life, because you have imagined it...you have *thought* it. Remain patient, and avoid becoming obsessive about your dream by wondering how long it will take or why it is taking so long. Being obsessive can push it away, and your dream will then be sabotaged by the old programming, beliefs and doubt in your brain. Allow your dream the freedom it needs to unfold in the best, most ideal way for you.

> *"Shoot for the moon. Even if you miss you will land among the stars."*
>
> Les Brown
> (American author, entrepreneur and motivational Speaker)

Every Powerful Thought You Have Gets You Closer

Once the exercise of creating your dream is complete, you may do as I did and put it away, deliberately releasing the dream for it to be fulfilled in its own time, fully expecting it to appear at any time. And it will. With subsequent knowledge and experience, I found that daily awareness of my thoughts and words helped my dream arrive sooner. Your new, specially chosen thoughts lift your life in each moment. You are making a choice to think and speak in terms of possibility from this moment on. This way your everyday words align with who you are already.

Everyone creates their life every day, whether they know it or not, but even when you are being deliberate, you must be aware that some deeper, unhelpful beliefs could shadow the result. The habit of complaining or expressing doubt will delay and confuse your dream. You are training your brain every day. Ensure your thoughts are ones that set you free. You have decided to be this person, so purposefully be them every day.

When You Need to Focus, Do it

Depending on your dream, there may be times when creating it takes you away from friends and family for a short time. You may need focus to achieve something specific, and distractions may block your dream. Trust yourself to be discerning about when you need to focus, and what you need to do to make your dream a reality.

Getting Out of Your Own Way

When you are on your path, it should unfold fairly harmoniously. If obstacles keep appearing, you may unintentionally be insisting on a certain outcome. For example, you may have your heart set on a house in a particular suburb, but you keep encountering barriers. Let it go, and you may find there is another suburb that better meets your needs. It can't come in, however, until you let go of the other suburb. Dream your dream, relax and assume that it is already done for you. Continue to act on opportunities as they appear. Notice them and express gratitude for them. You may be a little apprehensive about taking action, but be reassured that if each step brings you joy, then an amazing future is guaranteed. Enjoy the ride!

"Challenge is the core and the mainspring of all human activity.
If there's an ocean, we cross it;
if there's a disease, we cure it;
if there's a wrong, we right it;
if there's a record, we break it;
and finally, if there's a mountain, we climb it."

James Ramesy Ullman
(American writer and mountaineer, 1907–1971)

The World Benefits When You Follow Your Dreams

The only thing that can stop you from achieving your dreams and getting what you want is you. You are worthy of your dream, but it requires motivation and focus. The more people who choose to follow their dreams, the easier it is for others to do the same. Each person raises the frequency on Earth. You are raising the vibrations of the thoughts in the river of consciousness for others to follow. You can achieve anything you choose to do. Anything is possible. Follow any strong yearning to do something and you'll be helping Earth become a happier and more loving place.

Your dream is now in place. You and the quantum field know what you want. Move into your chosen future with confidence…and love every moment of your journey.

Summary of

"Creating Your Dreams"

♦   Everything in this world starts with an idea or a dream that someone imagines.

♦   If you have never considered what you want, that's why you haven't got what you want.

♦   By contemplating what you want, you can become clear about your goals, instead of changing your ideas every day.

♦   If you're dissatisfied with life but are unsure of what you want, your first goal is to know what you want. Establishing this takes you half way to achieving it.

♦   You must consciously create your dream if you want to experience your dream life.

♦   Congratulate yourself once your story is written. Celebrate your new life.

♦   Opportunities arrive on the heels of creating your story. Take action as they appear.

♦   Allow your dream the freedom it needs to unfold. Avoid becoming obsessive and wondering how or when it will arrive.

♦   Become aware of your everyday thoughts, and try to align them with your dream.

♦   It is important that you don't hold on too strongly to an exact end result, but instead allow all potentials to unfold. This way, your dream can be bigger than you imagined.

♦   As you follow your dreams, you add to the river of consciousness, you raise the frequency of Earth and you make it easier for others to follow their dreams.

CHAPTER 20

Creating Your Dream Career

*"Choose a job you love and you'll never have to work
a day in your life."*

Confucius
(Chinese thinker and social philosopher, 551–479 BC)

ulfilment comes from doing that which brings you joy and delight.[3] Your career plays a huge role in your life, and therefore in your happiness. The previous technique can be used to create your dream in any part of your life, including your job. However, we firstly need to get past certain beliefs some people have about earning money.

Wake Up Happy

So much time is invested in our work that it is an obvious necessity that, in order to be happy, your job aligns with your soul's desires. This is easier if you work for a business you enjoy representing – make it as easy as possible for you to have happy, higher thoughts. When you are happy in your job, there are so many advantages for you, your family and your community. Some people think they can't earn much doing what they want to do. This is true if that is what you believe, so cut out that idea. Your job should be inspiring and captivating. You should wake up looking forward to the day, and the start of the week should be gladly anticipated, not loathed.

"Do not lose hold of your dreams and aspirations. For if you do, you may still exist but you have ceased to live."

Henry David Thoreau
(American author and philosopher, 1817–1862)

Earning Money Should Be Fun

Most people have no expectation of being happy in their jobs, and this has become the norm. Complaining about jobs has become common in conversation. Most people think that as long as they are earning money, it is unlikely they will enjoy their job. Some are embarrassed about earning lots of money doing something they love; to them, it almost seems immoral to be having fun when everyone else is doing it tough.

When You're Happy and Don't Know It

On the other hand, someone may enjoy their job, but might have inadvertently slipped into a pattern of complaining about it – perhaps in order to be accepted by their friends. This is easy to do and easy to change. Some may also dread Mondays, but we need to remember that even enjoyable, fulfilling jobs require some type of discipline. Learning to be disciplined leads you to greatness. Consider whether you complain about a job you enjoy. If this resonates with you, contemplate why you do it. You may suddenly click into happiness when you recognize what you are doing.

When Convenience Edges Out Your Happiness

Some people feel unfulfilled in their job, but want to stay in it because it is convenient. If this is your situation, it is valuable to discover what holds you to the job, such as flexibility, more time with your family, or maybe it's close to home. If you can see the advantages in staying, there is a greater chance of appreciating and enjoying your job. Of course, there are always other jobs out there that provide similar convenience and greater fulfilment, but there needs to be a willingness to create that. If you decide to stay in a job for convenience, you should be aware that it was a deliberate choice to stay, despite other opportunities. Doing nothing is still a choice, but meanwhile, you can change your attitude to *gratitude*. An admirable attitude always brings more success in life.

"If nothing ever changed, there would be no butterflies."
Unknown

You Are Entitled to Be Happy in Your Job

If you are truly unhappy in your job, you may be staying for any one or more of several reasons. You may be unaware of your options, feel afraid that if you voluntarily leave a paying job, you are being unappreciative, or perhaps feel it is too risky to leave paid employment. Again, this is the body using survival tactics. It prevents you from creating a life you love.

Take the Easy Street to Your Dream Job

If fear is holding you back, expand your dream story to include the fact that your ideal job pays whatever you choose, and has always appeared in your life in the easiest way possible. This way, you are ensuring that your transition from your old life to a new one is as easy as possible...and why not? Have it happen smoothly and easily. Central to this theory, though, is that you still need the courage and willingness to alter your life, otherwise nothing happens.

The World Needs Your Talent

The direction you would like to take in your career isn't always obvious, but trust yourself – if you want it, the answer will appear. Everyone has numerous gifts that are unique to them. Endeavour to bring yours to light. Everything you love or love doing is a potential talent, and probably worthy of sharing with others. When you are daydreaming, consider all the things you love doing, or perhaps would love to try. Even crazy, seemingly unworkable ideas can be worth following to see where they lead, as they could be a key to finding your path.

How you could use your talents in a job isn't always obvious. For example, if you are a skilful organizer, then you may find project management appealing. If you are friendly with people, you may find a communications or liaison role attractive. You may require training to fulfil those roles, but the main thing is that you will enjoy the job. If you are unable to settle on one particular talent or direction, when you're writing your story about your dream job, include the fact that you have the necessary enthusiasm to find something. By including all the advantages of such a job, you are creating a job that you love, one that will serve you well. Again, intention works wonders.

There isn't necessarily just one idea or path for your life. Some people are born knowing what they want to do, and are happy sticking to that, but for others, it is important to follow many varied interests. As long as what you are doing is bringing you joy and delight, do it. If it isn't, change it. Explore different jobs, and ideas will unfold. The key is to keep learning and discovering more about yourself and life, continually keeping an open, inquiring mind.

Allow your talents to contribute to society and you'll have fun earning a living doing what you love.

Keep the Ball Rolling Toward Your Dream Job

"Nobody trips over mountains. It is the small pebble that causes you to stumble. Pass all the pebbles in your path and you will find you have crossed the mountain."

Unknown

Once you have created the story of your dream, then take whatever small steps you can toward it. As the opportunities start to appear, take action. Effort can sometimes equate to 'change' for the body, which makes it feel uncertain. Avoid letting a small amount of effort or slight apprehension keep you from your dream. Determination along with this effort should be all you need to make progress. Be sure to include in your story that you have the required determination to create your dream job. As you move forward, you will attract support from people and create events that you never imagined possible. Keep acknowledging even the simplest coincidences. For example, after I had been chatting to a friend about a new direction for her, she called the next day to say that a flyer on the topic had been

167

placed in her letterbox overnight. This all helps your acceptance that this is happening for *you*.

Your Dream Job is Being Arranged for You

Your first interview may or may not be the job you get or take, in fact you may attend several interviews without an offer, but always focus on your dream, and let the quantum field orchestrate the ideal job for you. Remember, there are infinite potentials. Ignore any doubts and remain firm in your focus that the best job is being arranged for you. If you have already had several interviews, treasure them as practice interview sessions that will provide valuable experience for when your dream job interview does arrive. Keep placing affirmations around your house and workplace, and always insist on the most powerful viewpoint.

Ensure You Are Fairly Paid

Be sure to get paid adequately, especially if you are self-employed. This way, you can continue to deliver a service that helps others, and you continue doing what keeps you happy. If you have your own business, people expect to pay you for the service that has helped them. Because there has been a fair exchange, they feel open to use your service again. If the service is free, or too cheap, people feel awkward; they feel that a balance is missing. Some may take advantage of you, but most people prefer win-win. Meanwhile, you will provide a greater service when you are being suitably rewarded.

Spreading Your Happiness Through Your Job

Your work, gifts and attitude will bring happiness to people. Dealing with you will be a special experience, and you will affect every person you meet. Happiness is easily spread. Your fulfilment will also take other people to a new level where they are then inspired to do what they love. It gives others belief and confidence, and they feel they have a right to fulfilment as well. You'll encourage them to think of possibilities; that, too, is a gift.

Your beautiful life is ready and waiting, detailed to your desires – so grab it. You can be happy all day, every day.

Summary of

"Creating Your Dream Career"

♦   Align your job with your soul's desires. We are more fulfilled when we do what we love. It becomes easier to have happy thoughts.

♦   There are several reasons why people are unhappy in their jobs:
   - There is no expectation to be happy in a job.
   - They may actually enjoy their job, yet slip into a pattern of complaining, perhaps to join in with friends.
   - They may stay with an unfulfilling job for reasons of convenience.
   - They may be unwilling to leave their current job because a new job is too much of an unknown, or they see leaving paid employment as being ungrateful.

♦   It can be a big step to leave your job and transition to a new, more fulfilling one. If so include it in your dream story as something that is easily done.

♦   You need courage and a willingness to make changes, or nothing will happen.

♦   It isn't always obvious how your talents can be used in a job. Start exploring jobs, and ideas will appear.

♦   It is healthy to change careers, as this way we keep learning, discovering and creating new experiences.

♦   As opportunities appear, be ready to take action to get your dream job.

♦   Maintain focus on your ideal job, even if it takes several interviews. Resist analyzing the situation. Stay inspired – the ideal job is on its way.

♦   Make sure you're paid adequately, especially if you're self-employed. Most people expect a fair exchange.

♦   As you do what you love, you bring happiness to yourself and others.

EXERCISE: How to Attract Your Dream Job

1. It can be challenging to leave the job you have and step into the unknown to follow a dream. This is especially so if yours is the main income in the family. If it is too challenging to make a clean break, you can start in the following ways.

2. Consciously acknowledge that you want to make a career or job change. Say to yourself, 'I am ready for a new career.' Until you signal this as a conscious intention, you can't start the process.

3. If you don't yet know what it is you want to do, work on noticing the ideas that pop up. Signal your intentions to the quantum field by saying, 'I know what I want to do and I am open to new ideas and opportunities.'

4. Whether you know your dream job or not, use the technique from Chapter 19 on *Creating Your Dreams* and describe your dream job as if you are already living it. Consider the secondary gains you will enjoy (these are the extra, often hidden, benefits you get from a job you love). This helps you get clear on what you want.

5. Once you've described your dream job, start investigating formal or informal study, reading different magazines, books or searching online job sites. Do anything to take action to get you closer to this new job, or at least closer to knowing what your ideal job looks like. One thing leads to another. Follow what feels like fun or is exciting. Do what you can as if you already have the job (identified or not), instead of waiting until you have it – keep the ideas moving. Waiting to find the right time in your life or waiting for something to happen usually means everything is stalled.

6. Once you have an intention to find a different job, you will find people and circumstances appearing to help you. Be open to how the ideas appear, e.g. you might be required to work unpaid for a period of time (on weekends/at night) in order to try something that interests you. Many people refuse to consider unpaid work, but this is limited thinking. If the thought of unpaid work leaves you feeling unmotivated, consider it a new experience, and as voluntary work, where

you are the beneficiary. If this is a dream and you are motivated to achieve it, be prepared to do whatever it takes. Keep in mind your objective of an ideal job, even if your path meanders and you have no idea where each opportunity takes you. A few sacrifices or a little extra effort along the way may be all that is needed to achieve your dream and change your life. If you choose not to do whatever it takes for this change in your life, then at least recognize that. This way, you'll still understand the power you have in your life.

7. Don't try to imagine *how* the next step or opportunity will appear and *what* the exact end result will be.

8. If you think it will be hard, it will be. If you think it will be easy, it will be. It is just as easy to put obstacles in your path as it is to find and expect the best solutions. Enjoy your wonderful dream and let it happen.

9. Create an intention to be grateful for what you have today, and enjoy every step of this journey. The more you do this, the quicker you create your ideal job.

CHAPTER 21

Letting Go of Control

"Control is never achieved when sought after directly. It is the surprising outcome of letting go."

James Arthur Ray
(American motivational speaker and author, b. 1957)

his book is about flying swiftly into the life of your dreams but, as with most things, there is a balance to consider. Although it's ideal to catch opportunities and use them to create your life, there is also a place to stand back lest you risk interfering with your dream by preventing the quantum field from delivering the best solution in the best way.

Over-Controlling is a Scarcity Attitude

If you attempt to over-control a situation, you hinder yourself and suppress your potential outcome. You may doubt your ability to get what you want, and believe you have to oversee every detail in order to get it, but being too controlling means you only see limited options – as if you are stuck in a small dark room. You become too focused and intent on one outcome, and miss out on myriad unseen potentials.

Trying too hard for an expected outcome, or expecting it to be delivered in a particular way, can hinder many areas of your life, such as finding the ideal partner, the ideal job, a certain type of healing, a new home, and so on. This is a scarcity attitude – thinking there is only one path, or one way of doing things, that there isn't enough to go around, that we must protect what we've got and fight for what we want. This doesn't sound like fun...it sounds like hard work.

For those who enjoy closely managing their environment, and for those impatiently demanding instant results, it can be a challenge to ease up on the controls. This is because the body feels safe when it is controlling its environment. However, the body only has a narrow viewpoint.

Letting Go is an Abundant Attitude

The fun way of getting what you want is called 'letting go' and it is similar to the freshness of viewing your possibilities from a mountaintop. It provides huge perspective and abundance. Letting go allows you access to all your potentials. It allows you to lift your head out of the small dark room to view all those exciting options you haven't yet imagined. You are raised to a higher frequency for greater results. Letting go expresses a desire to allow others to benefit from your success, it attracts and gathers everyone to you. You enable a collaborative society where everyone achieves their goals.

Letting go removes the body's limited viewpoint from the situation. Letting go is as much of an action as going for a job interview. It is different to giving up, becoming lazy or presumptuous. It is not apathy or inaction. You come to a point where you're confidently on your path to creating your goal and you are ready to harmoniously allow the quantum field freedom to supply it. When you let go, you allow the results to arrive sooner with a greater outcome. Create your goal and then become attuned to that stage when you must let go to allow it to happen.

When Your Results Aren't Obvious

Sometimes your results have arrived but you overlook them because they may be abstract or intangible. Changes are often beyond the body's comprehension. The body uses its senses – it must see it, hear it, or feel it and so on, so the changes often go by unnoticed. There can be disappointment that nothing happened. However there may have been an energy change, a deep inner healing, a subtle new way of thinking or you may have begun attracting the ideal people and opportunities – always some progress has been achieved.

Stay strong and motivated even if the results aren't obvious. If you do feel a little disheartened, then contemplate your progress by having the intention of finding several previously unseen results. If necessary, pretend they are there or try a new approach and ask yourself this instead: 'If progress has been made and there are results, how would I recognize them?' Changing the way you question yourself accesses a different part of the brain and you are open to other ways of thinking. The results are always there.

Letting Go With People to Get the Best Outcome

The need to control can be well hidden. Letting go is powerful, and by stepping up your awareness, you might find control existing in several areas of your life, such as in your relationships. Perhaps you want things done in a certain way, or need certain outcomes. This often happens in the workplace. When a manager delegates a task to an assistant, they should hand it over and then step aside. Micromanaging, or looking over the assistant's shoulder to ensure it is done the way the manager wants, limits the outcome and suppresses the development of the assistant.

Quite commonly, mothers are unable to allow fathers to care for their children. The mother will hover nearby, ensuring things are done her way, but if left alone, the father gives the children different experiences, and forms his own special bond with them in his own way.

Letting Go Opens Doors

Megan was in a rush to find a rental property. She set up the ideal outcome for the situation, and promptly found the ideal house. The estate agent said she could move in immediately if she wanted to. Megan was euphoric and left a message with the agent, but the agent didn't return her call. She kept ringing, but it seemed they were avoiding her. She was disappointed, and her first impulse was to nag the estate agent, but instead she reluctantly recognized that if it wasn't working out, there must be something even better out there. (Note: Megan let go of the idea of that house being 'the one'). She decided to continue viewing other houses and, as you may have guessed, the very next house she viewed, and rented, had not just one, but many aspects that were even more ideal to her situation.

Letting Go in Everyday Life

Even in minor situations, it's tough to let go.

We were halfway to the airport to meet a relative when we realized we had forgotten the electronic tag we needed for the toll road. We couldn't return home to collect it, because we'd be late for the plane. No tag meant inconvenience for us, as we would have to stop and buy a voucher, and we were already running late! We had assumed the tag was in the car, but we couldn't find it. It was a fairly minor predicament but, as often happens with couples, we blamed each other, and an uncomfortable silence followed.

I gradually became aware of what was happening. There was nothing I could do, but I vividly remember in that moment reluctantly letting the annoyance go and releasing the need to find this tag. (As often happens, I couldn't see a way out of the situation, so letting go was difficult.) Amazingly, in the *very instant* I let go, my husband once again lifted up the middle console where we had already looked, and the tag was suddenly visible, partly hidden by some CDs. My letting go had allowed me to see it – and yes, it was a huge relief.

I was aware that I had deliberately chosen to let go, and even in these little situations, I still get a buzz from such results.

Letting Go Reveals a Greater Destiny

Often our goals and dreams are *disguises* for where we are really heading. This is why it is important that we don't hold on too tightly to a precise end result, but instead allow all potentials to unfold.

175

It is the Jewel in the Crown

In *all* these instances, the quantum field is given the freedom to provide the best answer, the best path or best circumstances for you. Relinquishing control makes your journey easier, and provides a beautiful sense of freedom. It is open and gentle. You attract other people and unique circumstances to help you on your path.

Once you have tried it, you'll realize that it is actually a huge relief to let go. Once you've experienced its outstanding results, you'll finally accept that any potential and abundance is yours. You'll gain confidence to do it again. You'll start to see the wide, open freedom that is available to you, something that you've never allowed yourself to notice before. You confidently leave behind the small dark room of limited thinking, and step out and climb boldly upwards to stand on top of the mountain. You feel a richness of freedom and surrender washing over you – control has been cast aside. There is a power and radiance that shines from within when you open your life to all possibilities.

Letting go actually takes less effort than maintaining control, but it is nevertheless an intentional action. It is a matter of changing and opening your mind. The more you practice letting go and looking at that wide and open beautiful view, the greater and more astounding your results will be.

Summary of
"Letting Go of Control"

♦ There needs to be a balance between knowing when to put in the required effort to achieve your dream and knowing when to step back and allow the dream to unfold.

♦ Being over-controlling is limiting, and is the result of a scarcity attitude. Letting go enables greater perspective, additional options and abundance.

♦ Letting go is not about being lazy or giving up. Letting go is a deliberate action you take to allow your dream to arrive in the best way possible. You move away from expecting the outcome to arrive in a certain way, or to look a certain way.

◆   Sometimes you get results, but can't recognize them because they are intangible.

◆   The need to let go of control very often appears in our relationships with people, in the workplace and at home.

◆   Letting go of the outcome always enables a greater outcome.

EXERCISE: How to Start Letting Go in Daily Life

1.   Begin with awareness of the way you currently manage your life. Find out what causes you to control situations and you'll be more likely to detect those times when you are being controlling. It can be when you are feeling irritable, impatient or when you find yourself blaming others for incompetence. For a few days, try to notice whether you let situations unfold (let go), or whether you would rather decide each outcome and know what will happen (control it). If you feel tempted to control a situation or person, then acknowledge it and use the *Release Emotion Technique* (see Appendix A).

2.   Start with small situations. When you feel yourself starting to get anxious about how they will turn out, intentionally untangle yourself. Sit back and watch. Create a greater viewpoint by asking yourself whether the result really matters. Most of the time, you will gain perspective and be able to relax. Relaxing helps to create the best result, for both you and others.

3.   Notice the result. It probably worked out well for you, but if it didn't, then there is more to it, and the end result is still to come. Most times, the result will be better than expected. Your progress accelerates as you gain confidence at letting go.

4.   Congratulate yourself on letting go, even if you only did it for a little while!

CHAPTER 22

Letting Go to Reflect or Create

"In the attitude of silence the soul finds the path in a clearer light,and what is elusive and deceptive resolves itself into crystal clearness. Our life is a long and arduous quest after Truth."

Mahatma Gandhi
(Political and spiritual leader of India and the Indian Independence Movement, 1869–1948)

The body likes to be in control, and feels threatened when you ask it to merely contemplate. Contemplation means the body gives up its control. You may want to be quiet to listen to your innermost desires, but the body is more comfortable with the habit of constant survival mode mind chatter. Be strong enough to do whatever it takes to master your body, because once you are quiet, the body quickly succumbs, and you benefit from hearing those hidden messages.

Summary of

"Letting Go To Reflect"

♦   To have the freedom to reflect, you need to be strong so that the body releases its control over you.

♦   Recognize that the body has habits, and doesn't like change. New information and unusual requests make it uneasy.

♦   Keep finding ways to master your body.

EXERCISE: How to Let Go to Reflect

or Create

1.   If there is resistance, recognize the body's fears and be aware that it is not the real you that is resisting. Take steps that signal your intentions to your body, such as buying a journal especially for this purpose, or purchasing music you love and then making a date in your diary for a quiet time to listen. Use anything that will make your body feel that this will be a special event, and that it is safe.

2.   While many of us would enjoy something to eat or drink during these sessions, it's preferable that we abstain, because eating and drinking are tied into the body's senses, and can interfere with the meeting you're having with the real you. Initially, however, if you're able to get yourself over the line by promising yourself a cup of coffee or a glass of wine, do it. Do whatever it takes to achieve growth. Appease or engage the body just enough for it to follow your command, and then follow through on the intention. You'll soon know what works best for you.

3.   If sitting quietly is too great a request, decide on a walk, with the intention to reflect along the way. Again, do whatever it takes to get your body to do what you want. Once you have reflected while walking, the body will be more willing to reflect while sitting still.

4.   As you get closer to the time of reflection, your body may act up and resist the impending date. At this point, be firm

with yourself to get yourself over the line. Once you are sitting quietly, doing what you planned, your body will give in, and you will start enjoying it. Celebrate after the session, and thank your body for following through. While you are enthused, make another date for yourself, also accompanied by something that you enjoy. From this point on it gets easier, but you may still have to be firm with yourself.

Note: If you gave it a good go, but were unable to get yourself over the line, that's fine. Stick with it and make another date, perhaps changing something such as the location or the form of persuasion/reward.

CHAPTER 23

Letting Go of Your Past

"Those who stare at the past have their backs turned to the future."

Unknown

*W*hile the past should be cherished for creating who you are today, it no longer matters; it is finished. If you hang on to your past, you are not living today, and cannot enjoy your fabulous newly created reality.

You Are Recycling Your Emotion

According to quantum physics, everything is happening *now*... your past, present and future. This may sound incredibly weird, but remember this when you are tempted to discuss your past. Every time you speak of your past, you lose consciousness and are thrown back into that time. You get to experience that situation again...*now*. You are in whatever time you choose to place your focus. If the past involves pain, your body gets pummelled with the same distressing emotions all over again. This sounds awful, yet most people recycle the same emotions every day.

Your Past is an Emotional Addiction

Why, you ask? Past problems and their emotions can become addictive, because others listen to your story and give you sympathy or understanding. This makes you feel warm, loved and happier...for five minutes. Getting stuck in an addictive emotional cycle does not bring forward your dream life; instead, you get stuck in your past life, which eventually becomes boring – for you and for others.

For some, their past may be the highlight of their life so far. Re-living it helps them cope with today, but dwelling on it doesn't bring fulfilment and happiness today. It locks them in the past, they're absent for the vividness of today, and they're missing their bright future.

You only ever feel vibrant and alive in the *present* moment when you are *consciously* creating *new* experiences. Only your thoughts and experiences *right now* matter.

You Can Change Your Past

Agreed, the events of the past had a special purpose. They built wisdom, and allowed you to develop the motivation you now have to create awareness and a greater life. If your past was tough, and you feel you must go over it again, at the very least find some value from it. The value is there when you have an intention to find it. There are always several viewpoints to consider in any situation. This can change your opinion of the past, and it will reinforce the knowledge that everything you have ever done has helped you. As you change your opinion of your past, you are, in fact, *changing your past*. Spend a few moments releasing the emotion, and purposefully step out from the past forever and land into today feeling refreshed, enthusiastic and alert.

> "Let us not look back in anger, nor forward in fear, but
> around in awareness."
>
> James Thurber
> (American humorist and cartoonist, 1894–1961)

Keep Only the Wisdom...Forget the Rest

Society generally applauds the ability to remember every detail of the past with absolute clarity. As you relinquish your memories of the past and increasingly live in the present moment, some details you no longer need may be lost. If you are on a conscious journey of enlightenment, and find yourself unable to remember certain events from your past, then celebrate, instead of thinking it has something to do with old age. Age has nothing to do with it. This is different to losing your ability to use your brain, or losing your memory; those memories no longer serve a purpose. The pathways to that part of the brain have dissolved. This is what you want. You always retain the wisdom gained from your past, but it serves no purpose to engage in the specific emotional details.

Liken it to turning a ship around. With every higher thought you choose, you move closer to achieving critical mass and a chain reaction. You then face a bright new direction, and stand as a vibrant, empowered human being *today*.

Summary of
"Letting Go of the Past"

♦   If you hang on to your past, you are still living your past. Old experiences become boring. You are here for new experiences and new discoveries.

♦   Reviewing the aches and pains from the past means you re-live the emotion, and harm your body.

♦   Resist speaking of or thinking about your past. Stay in the moment. Always remember that you did your best in every situation, and that there are advantages in every situation.

♦   As you release the past, some of the detail will be forgotten. This is to be expected. Your memories are still as powerful as ever, but your focus has changed. The wisdom gained from every experience is always retained.

EXERCISE: How to Let Go of the Past

1.   The first step is to create an intention to
     - notice your patterns of thinking
     - release your past
2.   Notice *when* you usually dwell on the issues of your past, such as in the shower, driving your car, cooking dinner, walking the dog, and so on.

3. Your first step may be becoming aware of yourself reflecting on the past - you may suddenly 'wake up' while doing it. This is a good start.

4. Each time, quickly review the helpful aspects of that period of your life. Finding value creates a new view of the past, and you'll get closer each day to becoming more than your past.

5. To deal with unwanted thoughts, use the first suggestion listed in the exercise 'How to Consciously Choose Thoughts' in Chapter 3 *Whatever You Think Is True*.

6. Alternatively, you could use the *Release Emotion Technique* (see Appendix A). You are intentionally detaching from the emotion and releasing the energy of the experience. By doing this, you will ultimately cease thinking about that event.

7. Eventually you get to a point where your past fades away and there is less tendency to think about it. One day, you may even forget your past completely.

CHAPTER 24

Letting Go of Your Past to Transition to Your New Life

"Never look back unless you are planning to go that way."

Henry David Thoreau

(American author and philosopher, 1817–1862)

*P*eriods of confusion can occur even when you are on a purposeful journey of enlightenment. Creating goals means you're making changes in your life, and these can cause turmoil, strange feelings or even an absence of feelings. If you've never felt this, this chapter won't mean anything, but if you do ever feel numb, unsure of who you are or experience odd feelings, you'll think, 'It's great to know what's going on with me.'

You Are Making Way for the New

Once you have created your goals to get what you want, your brain and body need to be rearranged in order to achieve them. This means you need to release your old ways to enable the rewiring to occur. The old thoughts and patterns have to be let go. This can feel confusing, unsettling, and even create tiredness or illness. You may feel peculiar and disoriented, as if you don't know who you are any more.[9, 10]

It can be painful and sad for your body to shut the door on the past, and it may cause you to feel distressed and even depressed. Your body is struggling to say goodbye forever to a part of its identity. These strange feelings can occur suddenly at any time, even if, just the previous day, you felt inspired and empowered. This strange state is the result of being 'neither here nor there'. Not belonging or losing your identity can feel like anxiety or depression. It is similar when we travel – most of us are relieved to arrive at our destination, but being in transit can be disorienting.

This is the moment of your transition to a higher life, leaving the past and moving on to the future. Your new ways of thinking are fast becoming permanent in your life – they are no longer just potentials. At this point, the body may panic and try to hold on to the past by going back to old, familiar ways of thinking. It fights the changes by analyzing the emotion to work out why it's suddenly feeling different.[9, 10] It feels different because it's no longer its 'old' self.

Let Your Emotions Flow, Let Them Go

Resist the temptation to analyze the emotion, because you'll probably never work it out, and this just causes the emotion to get stuck in the body. If you are focusing on the emotion, you are holding it there, motionless. This extends the period of confusion, and can even block some of the reorganization. Give the emotions free reign while they are trying to come unstuck. Just *be* in the moment. Allowing them to flow lets them go.[9, 10] You can release whatever you are feeling without labelling it by using the *Release Emotion Technique* (see Appendix A).

Ah...Finally You Have Clarity and Meaning

As soon as you let go of the need to understand the process, relief is felt and the transition process is free to be completed more quickly. It is usually only a brief period of disorientation, but it depends – usually on what resistance there is within you, and on how large the change is. You'll know when the task is complete, as you'll feel new vibrancy, power, clarity and freedom. Your life will make even more sense.

This strange state is why some people give up changing their lives. They believe they should feel happy if they are thinking in an empowered way, and feelings of depression are unsettling. It's as if they are doing something wrong, and need to find answers elsewhere. It needs to be understood that this is a natural process. When it's over, the clarity and empowerment you experience makes it all worthwhile.

Even if you didn't have this information, the process would still take a little time, but eventually you'd feel lucid again…with added enthusiasm. Try to remember what has been discussed in this chapter to encourage you through the process and to *allow the changes to freely take full effect*. It is reassuring when you know what it is, and you can celebrate the fact that your focus and efforts are getting results.

Summary of

"Letting Go of Your Past to

Transition to Your New Life"

- You may experience periods of confusion on your journey to enlightenment.
- As we make changes, our brain and body require some rearranging.
- During the rearranging there is a feeling of being 'neither here nor there'.
- The body can panic and try to return to the old familiar ways, to its old identity.
- Whatever emotion you are feeling, let it be. Allow it to release itself, and avoid analyzing how you feel. The more you analyze, the more stuck you feel. Allow the energy to flow.
- Once you recognize this as a period of change, you will move through the process more quickly.
- When it's over, you experience greater clarity and empowerment and you can then celebrate your results.

EXERCISE: How to Let Go of Your Current Life to Transition to Your New Life

Keep reminding yourself throughout the day to stay present and to keep allowing the feelings to flow. Calmly allow yourself to feel strange. Submit to it. Just be in the moment. Understand that your old identity is being unravelled, and the new one is moving in. Reassure yourself that this is merely part of the process, and that the rewards are worth it.

CHAPTER 25

Letting Go by Being Honest

"Have the courage to say no. Have the courage to face the truth. Do the right thing because it is right. These are the magic keys to living your life with integrity."

W. Clement Stone
(Businessman, philanthropist and self-help author, 1902–2002)

Issues of honesty crop up in everyday events on the way to achieving your dream. How you handle them can accelerate your journey or slow it down. This is also known as acting with integrity. It's a touchy subject, because we all consider ourselves honest, yet as with everything, we are always improving. New situations may feel like uncharted territory. There are usually several angles to consider, and the right path isn't always obvious. Issues with integrity appear because the body loves instant gratification, it loves getting something for nothing and it has only a limited view of life.

Your conscience steers you in the most ideal direction. It's a gentle guidance from your soul, and provides an opportunity to create your ideal destiny.

We Are Taught That Minor Indiscretions Are Okay

Honesty is easier with an abundance attitude. We're more likely to be honest when we feel we already have enough.

By being honest you attract honesty, as well as the most suitable people and situations to enable you to achieve your dream. You are always more powerful when acting with integrity.

The best way to explain this is with examples, but ultimately, it becomes an inner sense, and you get more discerning with practice. Note that the examples below are usually seen as harmless and minor, and yet each attracts your future life to you. They teach us to choose integrity in the moment.

♦ Someone charges too low a price for an item at the checkout or hands us too much change. Do we tell them? People often think companies can afford that loss, but that isn't the point. If we notice the discrepancy, we should point it out. We shouldn't owe anyone anything. This way, we attract this behavior from others.

♦ Copying or buying pirate copies of games, CDs, DVDs and computer software is a contentious issue, as it has become a widely accepted activity. We can be tempted to blindly follow the pack, and there are many justifications, but no matter how we look at it, it is stealing. Is it okay for us because our friends do it? Those who copy software or who buy copied software set themselves up for having the same done to them. Everything has a consequence.

♦ Is it okay to use someone else's copied CD or DVD? Is honesty still involved, even when the copy belongs to someone else? Do we want to associate with dishonesty? Is there a limit to integrity?

♦ What about purchasing fake designer handbags and clothes. Some may say it provides employment for poor people, but what is it about the desire to own fake designer goods? Are we faking being wealthy? Is it important to us that others consider us wealthy, or that we create envy in others? What is the attraction of the label if the goods are false? If we can face being honest with ourselves, we learn a tremendous amount about who we are.

♦ Some people use the train without paying, or allow children in their care to get on without paying. They may consider it justified, feeling that the government owes them somehow, or they may simply enjoy beating the system, but our conscience knows. Expecting others to pay for us will not get us what we want. Similarly, some people only keep to the speed limit and stay sober in case they get caught, forgetting the important reasons for slowing down and being clear-headed behind the wheel. The more we take responsibility for ourselves, the less we need police to monitor behavior – allowing them to spend their time working on other matters that provide benefits for society.

♦   If we see an article or recipe in a magazine in a waiting room, do we copy it or rip out the page? Which is the right thing to do? Where do we draw the line? In the future people, may take something that belongs to us, and attempt to justify it.

You Attract Back What You Think and Do

This isn't about karma; this is simply about attracting the people and situations to what you think and do in your daily life...the frequencies with which you resonate. Note that it is vital to love yourself, regardless of whether or not you identify with any of the above examples. Your behavior merely serves as feedback for you. One of our purposes here is to become greater.

There is no right or wrong way to behave – the consequences will show you whether it is something you want to continue doing.

If in Doubt, Choose the Path of Higher Frequency

When in doubt, consider which approach provides you with the highest frequencies, and go from there. Remember though, the one-for-one correlation isn't always obvious – your behavior, what it attracts and how it plays out in your life may be puzzling. What we do know is that honesty always takes you directly to your dream.

Summary of

"Letting Go By Being Honest"

♦   We are constantly improving in all areas of our life, including honesty.

- The more honest you are, the more honesty you attract from people and circumstances.
- Honesty is linked to an abundance attitude. We're more likely to be honest when we feel we already have enough.
- If someone steals from us, it's not about finding fault or laying blame, but it can be an opportunity to review our life and contemplate how this situation came into our life. It is not good, or bad – it is all merely feedback for us.
- Love yourself regardless of what you find out about yourself. Your growth is fastest when you can be honest with yourself.

EXERCISE: How to Increase Honesty

1. Ask yourself, 'Which option best serves my integrity and attracts a higher frequency?'
2. You will get an answer, and in most everyday situations the answer comes easily, but the body may still be in favour of instant gratification, or tempted to get a bargain.
3. Even though we usually receive an answer immediately, the advantage of being honest may not be obvious. Sometimes it is a few hours or even days later that we will see why it was best we made that tough choice.
4. Your confidence increases each time you see this working for you.

CHAPTER 26

Patience

"Nature does not hurry, yet everything is accomplished."
Lao Tzu
(Chinese Taoist philosopher and founder of Taoism,
600–531 BC)

*P*atience is an *action* you take while creating your dream. Patience means several different things, depending on the circumstances. It means having perseverance and optimism, even when it seems nothing is happening or when something goes wrong. It means you calmly work toward your outcome, and allow it to unfold without being tempted to push for a result or act impulsively.

You Want it Now?

Generally, the body finds patience a challenge, as it prefers instant gratification, and waiting is considered demeaning. If things don't happen quickly, the body can lose interest.

For most of us, when we imagine something, it doesn't immediately appear in front of us. *But*, for now, that is a good thing. Imagine if you said something like, 'I'd die for a cookie right now', and the thought instantly manifested. We are protected from those thoughts, and until we are more responsible with our thoughts, we continue to manifest more slowly. The higher our thoughts, the higher we vibrate and the faster we manifest. Instant gratification is a gift we receive once the body has been mastered and the required wisdom and awareness are in place, but by then we are vastly different people with vastly different attitudes and perspectives.

You and Your Life Are Being Prepared

"Patience is the companion of wisdom."

Saint Augustine
(Philosopher and theologian, 354–430)

Progress is always being made toward your dream, but many aspects are intangible. You may be unaware that you are working on certain attitudes and skills to allow your dream to materialize. Circumstances are being unfolded and the appropriate people are being gathered to achieve your goal...all unseen and unknown to you.

But *Don't* Put Your Life on Hold

Patience is not, however, about putting your life on hold and waiting for results. Calmly maintain the usual flow of your life. Putting your life on hold can be compared to holding your breath or freezing the motion – it stops the flow of energy that creates your dream. It's similar to waiting for the phone to ring – it never does. If you think you need to halt your life and wait, your dream waits too. To ensure that your dream keeps unfolding and comes closer, proceed with taking advantage of opportunities as you would normally.

Never Give Up

Persist with your goals and dreams. Never give up. Focus on them every day in a detached way to avoid becoming obsessive or impatient. If your dreams are important enough to you, you will never give up. Every step on the path toward your dreams adds experience and wisdom.

Enjoy the *journey* toward your dream. The wisdom you gain on the journey is potentially more significant than the ultimate achievement of the dream, because that wisdom fills you with power for a greater life, and you keep it for all eternity.

Summary of
"Patience"

- ◆ The body loves instant gratification, and can lose interest if results take too long.
- ◆ Persist with your goals and understand that some results are intangible. You are constantly gaining experience and wisdom.
- ◆ Avoid putting your life on hold until there is a result. If you halt your life, your dream waits too.
- ◆ Never give up on your dreams.

EXERCISE: How to Develop Patience

1. If feelings of impatience arise, reflect on everything in your life for which you are grateful. This changes your perspective.
2. To improve your patience, when you create your dream, include smaller goals to keep you motivated along the way. Additionally, you may want to choose patience as one of your goals – by including it you are creating it. Set yourself review dates, as you would for a project at work. This helps the body to recognize progress and notice any intangible achievements.
3. Those smaller goals can be anything you do toward your goal. They may be very small, such as making phone calls, researching a new career or choosing a day to notice or improve an aspect of yourself. Achieving any small milestone is progress. Even the action of creating goals is progress. Noticing the smaller aspects of progress trains us in patience as well as in enjoying the journey.
4. Record your achievements in your special journal. This way, you add value to them, and it's a solid reminder of how far you have come. Your journal for your dreams helps make them feel sacred...your dreams and achievements *are* sacred.

CHAPTER 27

Laughing – It's the Best

"The one serious conviction that a man should have, is that nothing should be taken too seriously."

Samuel Butler
(English novelist, essayist and critic, 1835–1902)

*B*eing deliberate and determined on your journey requires a concentrated effort. It can feel like it's all work and no play remaining constantly aware, so be cheerful and kind to yourself on your journey. Cherish and encourage yourself, as you would a child.

There is No Good or Bad, it Just 'Is'

We talk about 'good' thoughts or 'higher' thoughts, but there is in fact no 'good' or 'bad' thought or situation.[3] One situation may be 'good' for one person but 'bad' for someone else. We decide whether it's good or bad through our filters.

Even though we try to be 'positive' in our thoughts and attitudes, in the quantum field everything really just 'is'; neither good nor bad. Therefore, try to allow any event to just 'be' somewhere in the middle. When we embark on this journey, there can be a tendency to get down on ourselves if we aren't making enough progress. You can change that. Changing your mind changes your world.

Seek Laughter

"The person who can bring the spirit of laughter into a room
is indeed blessed."

Bennett Cerf
(American Author, Publisher, Editor and Founder of Random House,
1898-1971)

By taking another look, many issues in your life will seem less serious. When we get caught up in our busy world, we can be deceived into thinking all our matters are serious.

While working in the corporate world, I needed a huge reality check upon leaving the building each evening. In the office, it sometimes seemed like there would be an outbreak of war or someone would die if we missed a deadline by one day. Once I was out of that consciousness, I came to realize how ridiculous the situation had become, and how I'd bought into it.

"When we laugh, experience a happy event or when we
exercise at a moderate level we decrease the chronic
release of cortisol and adrenalin and increase the release of
endorphins, enhancing the impact, the healthy effects on
the immune system."

Dr. Lee S. Berk
(Preventative care specialist and psychoneuroimmunology researcher
at Loma Linda University's Schools of Allied Health (SAHP)
and Medicine. *Source:* SuperConsciousness Magazine
May/June 2008)

Choose to seek laughter in people, movies, television or radio. Make it a priority to have a laugh. The more you laugh, the more laughter will find you. We live in a rather serious world, and we need to make a conscious effort to laugh, otherwise we get dragged down with the masses.

Know When to Hold 'Em, Know When to Fold 'Em
At first, it can seem like a lot of focus and effort is needed to become aware of your thoughts and attitudes, and you may

find yourself starting to plateau, or dragging your heels. If this happens, give yourself a break occasionally. People starting out on their path can temporarily lose their motivation if it's too intense. They need to give themselves permission to unwind for a while, and not care what they are thinking.

> *"Seven days without laughter makes one weak."*
>
> Anonymous

When I first started on a conscious path, I used to plateau and take up other interests. New interests that inspire you still get you what you want, but you can ease up on yourself about your thoughts. A breather may also be needed because you are embedding what you have already learnt, and need some time off to do this. When you are ready, you will gain renewed strength and motivation to go higher.

Of course, this isn't to be confused with a never-ending timeout. Be responsible for your journey. At some point, a little effort may be necessary to get going again, but you'll find that challenges will nudge you when it's time to refocus. Eventually, there comes a time when you won't need time off, and you will be inspired to constantly focus on awareness.

Life is to be enjoyed. Love yourself in every moment, no matter what you are doing or how you feel.

Summary of

"Laughing – It's the Best"

- ◆ There can be a tendency to get down on ourselves if we feel we are not making enough progress. However, everything just 'is' in the quantum field...neither good nor bad. Our interpretation of the world decides whether something is good or bad.
- ◆ Consider your life objectively, and you'll realize that we take much of our lives too seriously. Even small events can make us cranky. Seek laughter and fun in people, books, television and radio. The more you laugh, the more you will laugh.

♦ Learning to become aware of your thoughts and attitudes can bring a new seriousness to life. Take a break occasionally, and ease up on yourself. Life is to be enjoyed, and your growth will be jeopardized if you constantly need to whip yourself to keep going.

EXERCISE: How to Maintain a Light Heart

1. Re-evaluate the issues in your life, and gain perspective. If necessary, use the techniques from Chapter 5 *Challenges are Powerful Opportunities for You* and Chapter 12 *Making Your Own Decisions* to help you.
2. Surround yourself with light-hearted, inspiring people, and amusing movies, television and radio programs. Listen to uplifting music.
3. Read empowering, inspirational books.
4. Recognize when you need a break. If you're feeling frustrated, overwhelmed or overly critical of yourself, take a conscious break from creating your life. Yes, you will still be creating your life, but you will feel relief that you've given yourself permission to take time out. Be tuned in to when it is time to get yourself on track again – just as you would after a holiday from work.

CHAPTER 28

Humility

"To become truly great, one has to stand with people, not above them."

Charles de Montesquieuen
(French politician and philosopher, 1689–1755)

There is a saying, 'If you think you are humble then you are not.' The greater your personal power, the more important it is that you understand and strive for humility. Humility can be difficult to truly comprehend. The more humble you are, the more direct your path is to achieving your dream. Choosing humility in tough situations adds to your wisdom.

We're All Equal

As our knowledge and power grow, there can be a temptation to consider ourselves superior or more intelligent because of our achievements. This can creep into our attitude unnoticed, and it's often too subtle for us to detect in ourselves. We can get so involved in our achievements that humility is forgotten.

A greater level of awareness and high self-esteem helps us to stay humble alongside our achievements, otherwise an attitude of arrogance can develop, even in people who are on a journey of enlightenment. People can be lured into being proud, smug and unapproachable rather than being more understanding. Being constantly aware of humility is vitally important.

"Humility is the solid foundation of all virtues."

Confucius
(Chinese thinker and social philosopher, 551–479 BC)

What Does Success Mean Anyway?

It is unwise to judge another person's situation as less than your own. Often, a struggling person achieves greater wisdom and happiness in their time on Earth than the person living an 'easier' life. They have more to motivate them toward discovery and self-mastery, which of course creates wisdom and happiness.

Maintaining Modesty

It is common in organizations to see people who are unable to handle new positions of power with humility. Even small amounts of power can turn a modest, friendly person into a bossy, authoritative, arrogant monster. They've overlooked the nuances of life, whereby more is achieved through respect, recognition, collaboration, encouragement and motivation than through demands. When someone displays arrogance, it usually means they have low self-esteem.

While working at a large corporation, I noticed a colleague who was very aware of humility and the need to keep the focus on the team and away from her. Tina always tried to publicly recognize those staff who had the ideas and those who achieved, as well as those who did that extra special something, including displaying fabulous attitudes or overcoming obstacles. This motivated her team to do even more, because they knew they would get the credit instead of having it stolen by management (we all knew managers who were unable to resist the temptation to take all the glory). Tina found that she got recognition for the team's achievements anyway, and she had a happy team because everyone felt important. I saw how well this worked, and was inspired. Tina told me that the more the team achieved, the more she had to be aware of her humility. She knew the moment she lost her humility, the situation would fall apart.

Staying Focused and Grateful

Being humble means you are recognizing that your good fortune could have been otherwise had you had different genetics, less knowledge and wisdom and had made different choices. Humility keeps you focused on the need to take responsibility for your life, to continually create your dreams, and to humbly express gratitude when your dreams become reality.

The survival instinct of arrogance, superiority and winning is deeply embedded in our DNA. We have to intentionally move past that to greater attitudes. Modesty has far greater power to produce love, happiness and what we want than arrogance.

A reminder, again, if you have a strong urge to brag or behave arrogantly, do it. Experience it and when you sense the motivation to move on, you've now got the knowledge and tools to do so.

True Power Is Never Advertised

There is no need to advertise your power – people automatically detect it in you.

Summary of

"Humility"

- The greater our personal power, the greater the chance we may inadvertently consider ourselves to be better than others. This is an attitude that can sneak in without our noticing.

- Sometimes an attitude of arrogance can even develop in people striving for enlightenment.

- Humility means we recognize that our good fortune could have been otherwise, had we made different choices.

- Often, the person who is struggling in their life develops greater wisdom and happiness. They are more likely to be motivated to change their life, more so than someone in 'cruise-control' mode. Never judge another person's situation.

- The survival instinct of arrogance, superiority and winning is deeply embedded in our DNA, yet modesty has greater power to produce harmony, love and happiness.

- Arrogant people usually have low self-esteem.
- We are all equal; we merely choose different ways of living. Everyone deserves respect. The more we understand that, the greater our inner power.
- There is no need to publicize your power – people will automatically sense it in you.

EXERCISE: How to Recognize Moments

of Arrogance

Here are some clues to help you recognize if you are behaving in an arrogant manner. Most people display, or have displayed, moments of arrogance. The idea is to recognize it, and become aware of it. Once we have awareness of our thoughts, we can move to a new level of humility.

- Feeling aversion or contempt toward someone because they don't have what you have, or don't know what you know. This is when you consider yourself superior to others. Our goal may be to improve our opinion of ourselves and become greater, but we are never better than others.
- Feeling you deserve preferential treatment. We all deserve to be first, and the best at everything, nevertheless, it is up to each of us to create our own good fortune.
- Wanting to control others, and the way they live their lives.
- Boasting about your or your family's achievements.
- Considering yourself more intelligent than others.
- Being rude or disrespectful.
- Being presumptuous – taking too much for granted. Lacking in gratitude.

Section 5

Others in Your Life – Your Attitude Toward Them

"Kindness is difficult to give away because it keeps coming back."

Unknown

*W*hile monks choose to master themselves by staying away from others, the rest of us have chosen to master ourselves while managing our busy lives and interacting with a multitude of people. It's a matter of choice, but each has their challenges. In our day-to-day life, we have numerous distractions, a significant one being our relationships. It is part of our journey to manage these aspects. As we learn to be kind, accepting and helpful to others, we make our own journey easier and more direct, because we're looking into that reflection.

Your thoughts vibrate at a higher frequency once you do what you love, develop happiness and start getting what you want. All your thoughts are added to the universal mind – the river of thought and everyone accesses the universal mind.[3] The more thoughts of higher frequency that are available in the universal mind, the greater the potential to raise the frequency of everyone in the world. This assists others in your life, and the community senses it in a subconscious way, which leads to higher and higher levels of happiness in a community, just as teams experience a high when everyone is working well together.

We are all connected.[1] We are on this journey together.

The following chapters show you how your interactions with others can help you speed up the realization of your dreams.

CHAPTER 29

The Power and Freedom of Love

"A coward is incapable of exhibiting love; it is the prerogative of the brave."

Mahatma Gandhi
(Political and spiritual leader of India and the
Indian Independence Movement, 1869–1948)

*L*ove's tremendous power prevails every time when dealing with others. Add a little love, and you instantly enjoy a greater life. Love can easily be misunderstood, depending on your life experience. You may be suspicious of it, embrace it, or you may simply overlook its significance and the part it plays in your life.

It's no coincidence that we have the expressions, 'The power of love' and 'Love conquers all', yet many of us live each day unaware of the power we gain by ensuring that love exists in every part of our day. Love barely gets a mention in many societies, unless it is in the context of finding a partner, or vaguely muttering, 'I love you' to our family as we head off for the day.

Actively Encourage Love

Loving yourself has already been discussed as the foundation for your growth, and as a deep need for every human being. By acknowledging this, you can become aware of and appreciate the love you currently have. Consciously focus on love, and you will attract even more.

Love for others comes from loving yourself, and is a quick and effective way of increasing your power. You can create a fulfilling life just by focusing on love.

"Love is a force more formidable than any other. It is invisible - it cannot be seen or measured, yet it is powerful enough to transform you in a moment, and offer you more joy than any material possession could."

Barbara De Angelis
(American researcher on relationships and personal growth)

Love Transforms and Multiplies

Love is the essence of your being, and so you resonate with it and are drawn to it, usually without realizing it. This is why people want partners and want to have children. If you can achieve self-love, you are wonderfully self-sufficient. You may still choose a partner, but it isn't to 'get love'; it's to 'share love'. Love lifts everyone's frequency. It penetrates to the inner core of a person, and there is a transformation, even though we may not see it. Healing takes place every time a person experiences love. People resonate with love.

Show love, regardless of the person. Show love to someone, and both your lives are transformed. Love attracts more love, and is infinite. The more you share, the more you get back.

For some people, to show love is to feel a loss of control or power, and so to them love means weakness. Only the powerful can show love, especially during adversity or conflict. Why wait until somebody shows love to you, when you can start the circle. Even if the body squirms and struggles, you have the power to overcome it and handle any conflict with love. Start a circle of love, and it will eventually return to you *multiplied*.

As you experience the effects of love, you will understand its power.

Love's Challenges

When harmony reigns in our lives and we feel we are being treated fairly, it is easy to express love, and we enjoy helping others. The challenge arrives when we need to display love during adversity. This is understandable, but perhaps the term 'love' needs some explaining. To express love is to show yourself and others genuine patience, understanding, acceptance, gentleness, compassion, and so on, and it is during an altercation that the power of love is most effective.

Displaying love comes down to trust. When someone does something that is considered 'wrong', our initial instinct is often suspicion, mistrust and increased self-protection. If people have repeatedly been disappointed, their ability to trust is eroded. Since we mirror in others what we think, the behavior of other people confirms our suspicion (this also means we don't trust ourselves). The less we trust, the more people fail us. This way, we confirm to ourselves that other people cannot be trusted. What we think is always true.

You Are Rewarded When You Love

Love for ourselves naturally inspires us to shift this attitude to a higher level of believing in others, anticipating only the best from others, and trusting their intentions. We simply need a little courage to try it. We then reap the rewards as our lives get easier through attracting trust, along with other people who are drawn to help us. We no longer need to look over our shoulder all the time – people trust us, help us and want the best for us. We get a 'high' from love that is more permanent than the temporary addictive 'high' obtained from gossiping or finding fault with others. This is due to the magnificent rewards we receive from believing in people and living life every day in a loving, accepting way. This new high shouldn't be underestimated, as being proud of your choices is also hugely addictive. Furthermore, you powerfully and positively influence your community.

"Thousands of candles can be lit from a single candle, and the life of the candle will not be shortened. Happiness never decreases by being shared."

Buddha

Enjoy the Reflection

Love is free. There is nothing to gain by keeping your love inside, and everything to gain by sharing it. The fulfilment of your dreams and your enjoyment of them can only occur when you pour love into your heart, and from this oasis you get to enjoy the reflection of love from others.

Summary of

"The Power and Freedom of Love"

+ Love has tremendous power when dealing with others.
+ Recognizing the importance of love means you can treasure the love you have already and focus on it to attract even more.
+ Love for others can only start once you love yourself.
+ Everyone is affected, touched and changed by love. It lifts everyone's frequency. Healing takes place every time someone experiences love.
+ Love can completely transform an altercation.
+ Only the powerful can show love, especially during adversity or conflict.
+ Love is showing yourself and others genuine understanding, patience, gentleness, compassion, and so on.
+ We need a certain level of trust in humanity to show love. Trust can be eroded after we have been let down several times.
+ What we think, we attract. Therefore, the less we trust others, the more we attract doubtful situations, and the cycle continues. If we don't trust ourselves, we can't trust others, and they will let us down.
+ Love allows us to expect only the best from others, and to trust their intentions. As we move to an attitude of love, our life gets easier as we attract loving situations.
+ You have the power to start the circle of love and reap the rewards.
+ Love is free, and the more you give away, the more you get back.

EXERCISE: How to Focus on Love During Altercations

1. Learn to recognize if you have jumped to a conclusion. When two people disagree, it is highly likely both have valid points. Always endeavour to consider other points of view.

2. Assess whether you are suspicious as to the motives of the other person, i.e. are you expecting them to deceive you? If this is happening, and you've decided on a win-win solution, it's time to take a step back, soften your approach, encourage yourself to be objective and perhaps discover if you have your own hidden agenda or motives. You also need to change your mind to expect only the best from this person, and recognize that they are behaving to the best of their ability. A certain amount of humility is required at this point. View situations from a greater viewpoint, objectively and without fear, and situations will be solved more easily and harmoniously.

3. Practice recognizing interactions where power is at stake. For some people, a loss of power brings on anxiety and fear, as if the situation is threatening their survival. When people are in survival mode, they are likely to force situations to suit themselves, and potentially drive a wedge between themselves and other people. We achieve very little for ourselves when we operate from fear. Once you realize you are in survival mode, you are more likely to alter your approach to a more relaxing manner, perhaps by discussion and adopting a higher viewpoint, therefore achieving a better outcome for everyone.

EXERCISE: How to Add Love to Your Life

1. Take time during the day, or as you fall asleep at night, to reflect on the love you have in your life. The true blessing of love comes with being aware that you have it. By being aware of it, you are able to enjoy the warmth it brings to

your life. Noticing love brings more love, because you're increasing your focus on it.

2. As you fall asleep, also reflect on the parts of the day where you demonstrated love to others by being fair, considerate, friendly, helpful, understanding, patient, and so on. Bask in the glow of freely being able to add love to other people's lives.

CHAPTER 30

Kindness and Acceptance

*"Remember there's no such thing as a small act of kindness.
Every act creates a ripple with no logical end."*

Scott Adams
(American cartoonist, b. 1957)

As discussed earlier, kindness should only be expressed when it is freely given, with nothing expected in return. Awareness and a love of yourself enable you to do this, and you'll be blessed with extra-smooth sailing.

People undermine their good intentions by inadvertently creating the expectation of a return favour, and invariably feel let down as a result. Until you are ready to show kindness *unconditionally*, it is more fruitful for you to continue the work of loving yourself. If you show kindness prematurely, you open the potential for disappointment, and create obstacles on your path.

Kindness Comes from Unexpected Directions

There is a mystery to the inner workings of kindness. There is never a guarantee that your kindness will be returned by the same person, although it often happens this way. Here, the concept of 'letting go' appears again, as we realize that by allowing the quantum field to work its magic, it supplies us *endless* kindness from *all* directions…instead of the *one* place from which we expect it.

It starts very simply. While driving, if you give way to someone and they forget to thank you, allow that to be okay. You didn't do it to be thanked – you did it to be safe on the road. Was that achieved? Yes. *Your* actions are all that matter. You're creating your very own amazing world. Does it matter how kindness arrives? No. Keeping tabs on who has or hasn't returned kindness *blocks* the magic of the quantum field. It is a judgment to notice someone's lapse in returning kindness. This creates issues for you, as you will be attracting judgment and bitterness to you instead of kindness.

Keep in mind that most people do keep the flow of kindness going. Your kindness to them may have inspired them to be kind to another, instead of returning it directly to you. Your power starts the chain. Ultimately, however, it finds its way back to you…*multiplied.*

> *"When we seek to discover the best in others we somehow bring out the best in ourselves."*
>
> William Arthur Ward
> (American dedicated scholar, author, editor, pastor and teacher)

Minding Your Own Business

It is not your role to judge whether someone is playing their part or living up to your expectations. Accept people for who they are, because you can never tell what people are going through. They also have hidden fears or issues. We all do our best. It is plain simpler and easier to focus on your life. Let your reward be the pleasure of seeing someone lap up your kindness, and move on.

Kindness and Acceptance is a Gift to Others

Most people feel good through helping others. It doesn't take much to help, and in fact you don't actually have to 'do' very much. Generally, people just need acceptance. Kindness and acceptance are closely related. The more you create the life of your dreams, and the more you love and accept yourself, the more kind you automatically become to others. Showing kindness to others encourages them to accept themselves, and vice versa.

All People Smile in the Same Language

"Your smile will give you a positive countenance that will make people feel comfortable around you."

Les Brown

(American author, entrepreneur and motivational speaker)

Loving yourself allows kindness to filter through your entire day, even to strangers. It is no coincidence that a friendly face makes you feel great. An unexpected smile is always an enjoyable moment. You unknowingly change people's worlds, even if they don't smile back. A smile means you have noticed the person, and they are valued.

Your Gift Returns

As you accept others, despite their behavior, you give yourself the gift of acceptance. By choosing a friendly, accepting, kind approach, you are lavishly rewarded.

Summary of

"Kindness and Acceptance"

♦ The more you create your dream life and love yourself, the kinder you are to others.

♦ Only be kind if you expect nothing in return. Kindness will follow you anyway.

♦ If you show kindness whenever you can, the quantum field will reflect kindness to you from multiple directions. Never expect the kindness to be returned from the person you gave it to. This is a limited attitude. By letting go of this belief, you open yourself to kindness from infinite directions.

♦ Focus on your life and on how you can improve it, instead of examining other people's lives. Accept that other people make different choices to you for a variety of reasons.

♦ As you accept others, you are the one who gains acceptance.

EXERCISE: How to Show More Kindness
and Greater Acceptance

1. Become aware of your behavior when dealing with others. Are you patient and tolerant, or irritable, critical and cynical? If you wait patiently while a storeowner manages an unexpected situation, this is usually a pleasant surprise for them; customers like you can turn a tough day into a great day. Acts of kindness set the stage for attracting greater abundance, and when you leave that store you attract higher attitudes to yourself for the rest of the day. However, remember, do this only if you *want* to, and not because you *have* to. Don't do it to be accepted by others. If you don't want to be kind, don't.

2. Accept others for who they are. Do this by questioning whether you are perfect in all areas of your life, and whether it's possible that everyone's imperfections are different. While their imperfections possibly annoy you, is it also possible that yours annoy them? By being honest with yourself, you are more forgiving when others make mistakes, or when they don't behave as you would. Allow people to feel safe in showing you who they are. If you make a mistake, others are then also more likely to give you the benefit of the doubt.

3. Be an example to others; help them to believe that they can achieve any dream, and encourage them. Help them to see the world in a brighter way. Fill them with the hope of good things to come.

CHAPTER 31

Judging Others

"Allow the world to live as it chooses, and allow yourself to live as you choose."

Richard Bach
(American writer, author of Jonathan Livingston Seagull, b. 1936)

If you notice a 'fault' in someone, it means you have that fault too, otherwise you wouldn't even notice that aspect of the person. Your frequency resonates with that fault. This is the mirror situation at work again. There's just no getting away from it!

If you're judging others, you're distracting yourself; you're too busy criticizing instead of catching those fabulous opportunities that see you glide smoothly into your brilliant life. Getting past noticing faults in others is one huge step – in fact it's better than that. It's hundreds of *giant leaps* into your happy life. It is vital to your growth. When you can do this, you are truly flying.

Concentrate on Your Life

The things you like and dislike about others are the same things you like and dislike about yourself. When you discuss others, you are essentially talking about yourself.[3] It can be a challenge to face this truth, and it takes courage to have sufficient honesty to do so. Take it slowly. As always, though, there is something marvellous in it for you.

216

Recognize that everyone views faults in a different way, because we filter our worlds differently. Nevertheless, there is never a reason to find fault, because other people's lives are none of your business. You only hurt yourself by doing this. As there is no 'right' or 'wrong', the only value you get from noticing a fault is the opportunity to recognize what you need to work on within yourself. It is a key to your growth to overcome judgment of others, and instead use what you are tempted to criticize as feedback for yourself. Remember to love and accept yourself through this process.

> "When you judge another, you do not define them, you define yourself."
>
> Wayne Dyer
> (American motivational speaker and author of self-help books, b. 1940)

Idle Chatter Hurts You

Become aware of gossip. Most people are unaware of the ramifications of gossip, because it feels good...for a short time.

If you talk about someone's behavior, you magnetically attract that behavior to you, be it pleasant or otherwise. Our criticism attracts criticism from others, which is painful for us. The more we criticize others, the more neurons in our brain focus on dissatisfaction, which in turn leads us to feeling bitter about life. Whatever you judge in others, you invite into your life (this is what you are *thinking*), therefore you face the faults you find. You attract unkind behavior and unhappy people. By judging others, you lock yourself into a prison. This is because judging others creates awful rules that you must then follow, or risk being judged. Throw away those rules, and you'll be throwing open the doors of freedom for all.

Incidentally, if you're wondering about those group situations where everyone thinks a particular person is nasty/unhelpful/annoying, you may be thinking, 'Well then, everyone has this same issue', and you'd be right. Remember, friends think in similar ways – that's why they are friends. In addition to taking a look at yourself, turn again to quantum physics for an answer. There are infinite timelines on the quantum field, and each timeline is a different potential. All it takes is for you to choose one where you get along with this person, and before you know it, you do. If you want it, you can have it. The other people in the group may still have the same issue with that person, but you? You've shifted timelines. Well done!

Criticizing can be so habitual that it is hard to detect, so you need to gradually build an awareness of it. It can easily escape conscious awareness, and then you unintentionally get entangled in someone's gossip session. Generally, it is best to completely avoid talking about anyone.

Allow others the peace to live their lives in the best way they can, and you will receive the same gift in return.

We're All Doing Our Best

When we observe others behaving in ways we wouldn't, remember; they're doing their best. They may not have the awareness or life experience to do better. Your only reaction is to *be grateful* that you have a greater ability, and to remember that this ability may be important to you, but not to them.

> "To find fault is easy, to do better may be difficult."
>
> Plutarch
> (Greek historian, biographer and essayist, 46–119 AD)

A friend of mine, Jack, had an excellent sense of direction and would become irritable and frustrated with people who couldn't read maps. In circumstances such as these, we should be thankful for our ability without comparing it to that of others.

Celebrate Your Differences

Further to this, understand that everyone has different talents, so they may excel in some parts of their lives and yet need to work on others (according to you of course). One person may be friendly and helpful to others, yet they are often running late. Someone may have a very untidy house, yet they have a heart of gold, making everyone feel warm and welcome. We all have our own unique, remarkable abilities, and other areas that need improvement.

Allow others to choose their lives. We are all attracted by opportunities that help us grow, and we should grant everyone the freedom to choose their path.

Every Situation Is Progress Toward Your Prize

Create an intention to notice when you are tempted to judge. If you sense an injustice or try to argue a point, it's a good time to assess the bigger picture. At first, you may not be able to stop yourself, but at least you noticed it. High-five yourself. There comes a day when you can stop yourself before you say anything, and then there comes the day when you acquire the art of embracing people for who they are. Use every situation as an opportunity to learn about yourself. Your prize is that people completely embrace and love you for who you are, because you vibrate at the frequency of acceptance, and you luxuriate in their brilliant reflection.

Honesty Takes Courage

As always, go easy on yourself as you work on this. Take what you are tempted to judge, and look within. Be proud that you want to learn, and that you are seeing who you really are. The world is filled with people who judge others, and we are all where we should be. It is an exceptional person who can be honest with themselves in this regard.

Anything Goes

Others will always do things differently to us. Allow them to do so. When you cease to judge, you are no longer judged.

Summary of

"Judging Others"

- Noticing a 'fault' in someone means you also have that same 'fault'.
- Instead of judging others, notice what you are tempted to judge and look within, so you can learn about yourself.
- Whatever you judge in others you invite into your life, therefore you experience the effects of your judgment. If you judge, you attract criticism and bitterness, and put yourself on a path to unhappiness.
- You can understand others more if you realize that most people behave to the best of their ability.

- Your focus shouldn't be on others; it should be on developing yourself to be the best you can be.
- Everyone has different talents, and while we excel in some parts of our lives, we need to work on others. When you criticize others, you forget that you are also working on certain areas.
- Being critical becomes a habit. Learn to catch yourself being critical and as you do so, you can learn something about yourself.
- When you overcome judgment of others, you get more help to achieve your dream.
- Be kind to yourself throughout this process. Whatever you notice about yourself, love it – love yourself beyond your behavior.

EXERCISE: What You Can Do to Accept Others as They Are

1. Use the faults you notice in others as an insight into those areas of yourself that need release. As you gain the understanding of seeing yourself in others, you handle others with more compassion, and you accept them with greater ease and understanding. Accepting others helps you to accept yourself. If you find an area in yourself requiring growth, celebrate rather than feeling ashamed, guilty or annoyed. It exists whether you like it or not, so it becomes your opportunity to release that aspect forever. Face it. Constantly tell yourself how wonderful you are, and how well you are doing. You gain a greater realization that we are all here handling life in the best way we can.
2. Even the most kind-hearted groups of people bond by discussing other people. It's corruptive, however, and we need to be strong enough to refrain from participating. Become aware of when people are complaining about others, and then either stay out of it or approach the situation with humility and do what you can to balance the discussion by highlighting their strong points.

3.   When people discuss their lives with you, keep it to yourself. Resist the temptation to talk about other people's lives, regardless of whether it is considered good or bad news.

CHAPTER 32

Forgiveness

"To forgive is to set a prisoner free and discover that the prisoner was you."

Lewis B. Smedes

(Author, ethicist and theologian, 1921–2002)

There is *nothing* to forgive in another person, ever.

Most people have at some stage found themselves at odds with another person, and felt betrayed or deceived. The brain and body get flooded with thoughts of hate and revenge. The body feels almost ill. A part of us is aware that we should forgive, but another part wants revenge and justice, and the result is a tangled web of confusion. We go round in circles instead of heading off in the direction of our dream. Our dream is put on hold. Unresolved tension with others can have serious harmful effects in many areas of your life, including health.

Thoughtlessness and betrayal do *not* exist. This may be a challenge to comprehend, but they can only exist if you want them to, and if you buy into the habit of self-pity. This serves no purpose, and blocks your path.

The good news is, there is an easier way!

Shift the Power from Them to You

Once again, it is a learning opportunity for you, and once again, every situation is simply feedback for you. This means more power for you, which simplifies your life, because you are removing the complication of everyone else and focusing on yourself instead. It is a flick of a switch in your brain from them over to *you*, and when you do this, the power shifts from them to *you* – where it belongs.

Avoid Getting Stuck in the Mud of Justice

Many thoughts and conversations involve blaming others for our life, and most people consider blame to be an acceptable coping method. It momentarily makes us feel good to blame others for hurting us, because it absolves us from responsibility. We feel liberated in that fleeting moment, but this is a deception. When we blame others, we create a prison for ourselves. We lock ourselves in a holding pattern, looking for revenge and justice, and we give away our power. If revenge or justice is never achieved, we stay locked up, trapped *in that moment* in our lives (in our past). As the days go by, we blame more people and we get more frustrated and confused. Every day, we live with churning thoughts of hate and revenge, constantly attracting more of it.

The very instant you genuinely release people from blame, you are set free to get what you want. When you free others, you are instantly free. *One simple change of the mind* – it's that easy.

"Nobody can hurt me without my permission."

Mahatma Gandhi
(Political and spiritual leader of India and the Indian Independence Movement, 1869–1948)

Who Is Pulling Your Strings?

Certainly, other people's behavior can be perceived as insensitive and hurtful, but blaming others puts us at the mercy of *their* behavior. By saying someone hurt you, you are allowing *their* behavior to *push your buttons* and *affect your emotions*. This really means *you let others control you. They* decide when you will be happy and when you will be sad. This keeps you on a never-ending roller-coaster of confusion about your life. Surely *you want control* of your emotions, regardless of someone else's behavior? The more you take charge of your life and take responsibility for your interactions, the less likely it is that you will get hurt. Avoid helplessly waiting for others to behave so you can be happy.

As you grasp this knowledge, you become more considerate and tolerant, and you ignite the power in your life. The pieces start to fall into place, and there is an uplifting relief at not being at the mercy of others, at the realization that people are not out to get you and that you have freedom to decide how you handle every situation.

Nothing is as it Seems

People are rarely objective about situations, especially when they are emotional, tired, hungry, etc. They cannot see both sides of the story, nor do they want to. If an explanation was provided under normal calm circumstances, everyone involved would feel validated, and would usually quickly see that no harm was meant.

The emotion left over from similar past experiences can trigger an involuntary intense reaction. To avoid reflex reactions in future, these emotions need to be acknowledged and released as soon as you experience them. Once they have been released, if the same situation were to happen again, there would be little or no reaction, even if one were tired, etc. At the very least, if you can't immediately interpret the message for yourself, acknowledge that it is nothing to do with the other person. Release them, and your power increases.

Use it as a Precious Teaching For You

Use the opportunity and ask yourself what you can learn from looking into the mirror of that person. At this stage, there can be a temptation to switch from blaming others to blaming yourself, which also misses the point. Some people feel lost once they can't blame someone else. It can shake their understanding of the world. This is where knowledge helps. We are here to master ourselves, to master our reactions to life and to do it in a loving manner – to leave 'fault' or 'blame' out of it. Leave 'good' and 'bad' out of it. Admittedly, all situations could be handled better, or differently, but then, all situations can be viewed differently, too. It is not punishment; it is merely feedback for you – and only you.

The feedback purely helps you learn how to take control of your life. Taking responsibility for your emotions and your life has nothing to do with finding fault and everything to do with gaining wisdom.

The Truth Is Painful but Living a Lie Is Worse

Once you accept that you cannot know for sure the motivation of another person, you avoid the endless analysis of why it happened. All situations help you gain a greater understanding about life. If someone chose you to be part of their experience and it hurt you, then you attracted them to your life for your own learning. It's that innocent, and that simple.

While you attract these situations to you, the person you are dealing with is probably struggling just as much as you are. Often, they are operating from a position of survival, and are unaware of their behavior, although we must be clear; if you are involved, you *attracted* their behavior. No ifs or buts. Blame and revenge only makes us feel good temporarily through the addiction of self-pity. Remove the person from the situation. They are simply acting as your messenger.

Seeing your thoughts coming to life via the behavior of another person helps shed light on how you think. In seeing them, you are watching your own thoughts and attitudes happen. You can choose to learn from the reflection. It may hurt, but this isn't the intention. The quantum field is merely reflecting your thoughts, and this usually shows up in other people. If you think someone hurt you, then look within and consider how this situation reflects who you are – perhaps you do these things to yourself, or to others. Perhaps deep down, your thoughts are that you feel unworthy, and that you deserve to be treated like this. Say to yourself, 'I get it; I accept that this is my reflection.' Sometimes, this is enough. Only you can discover why you create hurtful events in your life – the possibilities can be weird and infinite. The answer lies within you, and only you can discover the answer. Do whatever it takes to find it, and then you can release it.

The reality and truth about yourself can be painful, but living a lie is worse.

Break Free From Blame

Once you see blame for what it is, you are given a gift of freedom. Freedom is priceless, and propels you to greatness. Life is easier, simpler and more empowering.

> *"Whenever you're in conflict with someone, there is one factor that can make the difference between damaging your relationship and deepening it. That factor is attitude."*
>
> William James
> (American philosopher and psychologist, 1842–1910)

Here is a situation involving forgiveness that I encountered many years ago. At the time, it was a significant teaching for me.

My daughter was a member of an athletics team, and she needed to attend a competition for a few days in a rural town. As it was a long drive, my friend and I, along with several of the mothers, decided to travel by car in convoy.

The night before returning home, we agreed to meet in the dining room for breakfast at 8 am the next morning and then travel home together.

At 7 am the next morning, my daughter and I were in the middle of packing when there was a knock at the door. It was my friend. She told me they had already packed their cars, and everyone was leaving. I panicked and said I was still packing and couldn't leave yet. She apologized, but bluntly said they were leaving at once. I felt completely shocked and bewildered...as if I had been punched in the stomach. I closed the door and my daughter and I watched through the window in disbelief as the other cars left, and we then went to breakfast. I felt totally abandoned.

Once I got home and felt calm, I chose to call my friend to tell her how disappointed I was. She seemed her usual cheerful self, and obviously did not think she had done anything wrong. Even though I was hurt, I knew that this situation had some meaning for me. It took me several months of inner searching to discover my message. One day, during a time of contemplation, I received the answer. As so often happens, my message was actually quite simple, even though it took so long to find.

Over the past several years, I had chosen to be more by myself, and I now realized that this choice had simply been reflected back to me. I enjoyed my own company, and loved to write, read and study. I had chosen to stay on the periphery of this type of group, and tended to prefer one-on-one friendships. This experience had shown me who I had become. I had chosen to be excluded from this type of group. Still, it was one thing to be living the life I wanted, but quite another to have it reflected back to me! To see my thoughts played out in vivid colour had been a shock, and definitely wasn't pleasant.

Once I grasped the message, I was able to embrace who I had become. I understood the consequences of my choices, but I was still happy with them, so I didn't change anything.

My friend and the rest of the group were blameless. They had merely reflected to me who I was. I did not resonate with this group, so I was excluded. They acted in accordance with who I was. It was nothing more. No malice, nothing…just a mirror. I contemplated my *reaction* to the incident, which demonstrated my need to be included, and took the opportunity to own and release those emotions. If a similar situation occurred in future (it did), it would test whether I had completely released those emotions (I had). If I had successfully released them, then in a similar situation, I would open the door at 7 am and hear my friend's news without reaction – it would be the most normal, acceptable thing to hear.

It's not about life getting back at us; it merely reflects exactly what we are thinking. The quantum field acts like a mirror – this is who you are. If you like it, great; if you don't, you have the freedom to change it.

If you ever feel emotions you don't want, it is a wonderful clue that you need to release them. Being aware of them means they are ready for release. Keeping them is futile – they damage your body and block your growth and happiness.

Some people experience similar situations and hold a grudge for years, sometimes even forever. They harm themselves every day physically and mentally, because the thought of revenge remains unresolved in some part of their brain. They resonate with revenge, therefore they continue to invite similar issues. Always try to release the person, and be open to receiving your message.

> *"The weak can never forgive. Forgiveness is the attribute of the strong."*
>
> Mahatma Gandhi
> (Political and spiritual leader of India and the Indian Independence Movement, 1869–1948)

You Experience a Beautiful Sense of Loving Yourself

Acknowledging your responsibility in this *is so beneficial* that you could almost think of it as selfish. By letting go of the other person and rising above the situation, you experience a beautiful sense of loving yourself – and others. You are providing a wonderful contribution to yourself and humanity. Isn't it better to be empowered and choose your emotions, rather than being a victim of those around you?

Disputes Clear the Air

Remember, too, that life works in mysterious ways. A dispute with someone close to you can actually be instrumental in bringing you closer together or helping you to work better together – if you choose for it to be so. It can be healing for both people. You will understand each other better, and have a more open communication. You may both discover a deeper issue you never knew you had. You'll be the bigger person by putting the survival attitude aside, resisting retaliation and choosing to view the situation from a higher perspective. You'll feel liberated and fulfilled by acting with integrity.

> *"Forgiveness is the key to action and freedom."*
>
> Hannah Arendt
> (German-born American philosopher and political scientist, 1906–1975)

Avoid Playing 'God' in Other People's Lives

Your role in life is to learn who you are, and you are the only one you can change.

If you are new to forgiveness, it can help to talk to the person about it, but, as in my previous example, they may not even realize what they did or that it hurt you. You'll also realize that letting them know they hurt you really makes *no* actual difference to your life. It isn't our job to teach others appropriate behavior, or to decide who deserves what lesson. Other people learn through their own special life lessons and feedback – just as we do.

Stop Allowing Others to Imprison You in Your Past

You are the one who decides if it is time to release any such aspects of yourself. There is no need to know why you have the issue or emotion; you merely need an intention to heal and move on. Do your best to be honest with yourself and, as always, remember to love yourself.

If you choose retaliation or blame, you will continue to find the world a hostile place. No person or situation is worth that. By allowing a person to forever stand in the way of your growth and happiness, you are handing them the power to imprison you in your past with all your emotions, be they friends, family or strangers. Never allow others to hold you back and control your life. Release blame. It may be uncomfortable at first, but eventually, you'll probably find it is tempting to choose freedom. Use the *Release Emotion Technique* (see Appendix A).

You Are Where You Need to Be

Then again, if you're not ready to release others and accept responsibility at this moment, that's fine. If you still prefer retaliation or blame, that too is okay. Everything is okay – you are where you need to be and must experience what you are drawn to. There are always consequences, but at least you will have a greater understanding about what is happening. You now have this knowledge, and a seed has been planted. You have already grown, and there will come a day when you are ready to accept responsibility. Be gentle and patient with yourself. Use new knowledge when you are ready, and when that moment comes, you'll hardly need to make any effort.

Work On One Situation at a Time

The first time you try being objective in a conflict, you may feel a mixture of acceptance, anger and blame, but you are trying, so do the victory lap anyway. The temptation for revenge can be very strong. Revenge and blame create a delicious feeling in the body – even a sense of power – but it is temporary, like any addiction. This is normal. Be strong to resist and overcome it. It is through taking action, even small steps, that you improve and gain awareness. Each attempt means new pathways are built in the brain – pathways to taking responsibility for your life, to choosing growth and freedom over past emotion and imprisonment. Those pathways are made stronger each time you try the new way of thinking. Celebrate every attempt, and every time you overcome the temptations of the body.

Through forgiveness, you are free to continue your path of getting what you want, you are free to follow your heart and you add wisdom and happiness to your life.

Summary of
"Forgiveness"

♦ There is nothing to forgive in another person, ever. The situation is merely a learning opportunity for you.

♦ If you blame others, you are putting yourself at the mercy of their behavior. You shouldn't allow others to control how you feel.

♦ When we blame others, we create a prison for ourselves, and we put our lives on hold waiting for justice. Some people wait their entire life for justice that never comes.

♦ How empowered are we if we depend on others to make us happy?

♦ Thoughts of betrayal and revenge stem from feelings of self-pity, and this gives away our power.

♦ We need to leave out whose 'fault' it is. It isn't their fault, and it isn't our fault. The situation is neither 'good' nor 'bad'. The other person is simply our reflection.

- People usually have no idea why they behave the way they do. It is best to leave the person out of it and contemplate what we can learn about ourselves from the situation.
- If you allow a person to forever stand in the way of your growth and happiness, then you are giving them the power to imprison you in your past with all your emotions. You will not find what you want in your past.
- Your thoughts attracted the situation, you attracted the circumstance…it belongs to you. The experience is yours to use – if you so choose.
- Only you can contemplate yourself and figure out why you create undesirable situations.
- Tell yourself, 'I get it; I recognize that this is my reflection.' This may be all that is necessary for you to release the other person.
- You will only find the meaning if you are honest with yourself, which can be the toughest part. Often, we are our biggest critics, which is why we must be sure to give ourselves love and reassurance every step of the way.
- You give yourself freedom when you release the involvement of other people.
- Once you see and accept blame for what it is, you are free. You are free to move on and create your greatest potential.
- Every time you approach a situation as objectively as you can, new pathways are built in the brain, and each time it is easier for you to take responsibility for your life and to gain more freedom.

EXERCISE: How to Release Others From Blame and Revenge

1. In most situations, a discussion with the other person is unnecessary, and they may not even want to talk about it. If you absolutely need this to move on, then by all means proceed. All you really need is honesty with yourself and a willingness to learn and move on. Many of us believe feedback will help the other person, however we are not

responsible for their teaching. If for some reason you feel it is important that they reach an understanding, that is the time to rely on your communication skills. However, only discuss the problem, avoid blame, and avoid discussing their personality. Act with humility, and try to discover the other person's intentions or concerns, recognizing that they may have issues with you, too. None of us is perfect, and the aim of the discussion is to work through the situation to achieve harmony – not the upper hand.

2. If someone annoys or hurts you, say to yourself, 'I accept this as a teaching for me; I am able to understand myself more by seeing my reflection in others, and I release them.' You may feel as if you are pretending, but what you imagine and the words you say are real to your brain. It believes them, and your God creates your life unquestioningly according to your thoughts. Therefore, you will naturally start developing greater acceptance of others and improved relationships.

3. Contemplate the message/reflection in the situation. Do this either by asking yourself or by imagining a conversation with yourself sitting next to you. Consider how your thoughts, attitude and behavior could have created this. By being deeply honest, and with the intention to do so, you can recognize the reflection your life has created. What views do you have about yourself that allows them to make you feel bad or sad? If you feel unable to get the message, simply tell yourself that you are ready to know the answer to this, no matter how hard it is to accept. Over the next few hours, days or weeks you will get your answer, but you must be open to receiving it, otherwise you won't recognize it. At the same time, if the answer doesn't seem to be coming, choose to release those emotions using the *Release Emotion Technique* (see Appendix A). The intention to take responsibility is what is most important. Remember, it is not about blaming yourself, either.

4. Ask yourself if you may have done something similar in another circumstance involving someone else. This is not to create guilt or to find fault with ourselves. Viewing the situation from this angle may or may not find your answer,

but it helps you to understand others and go easier on them, and to find your reflection.

5. Consider your beliefs and opinions about life. If you believe 'bad' things happen, then they do. Contemplate what you believe to be true about life. This may lead you to your answer. If you find a belief that isn't helpful, you'll be able to start changing it.

A Forgiveness Exercise

(This exercise is based on the work of Doreen Virtue, author of *Healing with Angels*. Doreen also credits the author John Randolph Price.)

1. List all the people, living or deceased, with whom you've ever had any issues. Include anyone who has ever annoyed you, even strangers. You will be amazed at how many names you write down. Include your own name.

2. When you have an hour alone, move through the list one at a time. Remember the person, and say to them, as if you were face to face, 'I now completely release you.' Be present with them.

3. On a telepathic level, they get the message, and will detect a greater freedom. You release them, and instantly release yourself.

4. It is important to complete the list, even if it gets a little tiring by the end. You will feel a magnificent peace and freedom.

You will have done a beautiful deed for yourself and humanity. Everyone on Earth, including you and each person on your list, benefits from your forgiveness.

CHAPTER 33

Saving Others from Their Challenges

"People take different roads seeking fulfilment and happiness. Just because they are not on your road doesn't mean they've gotten lost."

H. Jackson Brown, Jr
(Author of Life's Little Instruction Book)

Suppose you had a situation where someone close to you was in a pickle and you could take all their 'troubles' away. Would you do it?

Although tempting, it is not appropriate to 'save' someone from a challenging situation, especially if they haven't recognized the signs of what's happening to them. You would be interfering. Your purpose is to focus on y*our* dream, y*our* growth and getting what *you* want. Strange as it may seem, it is in this way that you help others the most. Saving others is not only *not* part of your purpose, it also takes you away from your goals. You can still empathize with them and continue to accept, love and support them, but resist taking away what looks like 'troubles' to you. Their life is not your responsibility. People are where they should be; it is ideal for them, and they are gaining wisdom. It may be uncomfortable for them, and it may be distressing to see them struggling or confused, but they are at an ideal stage for their growth.

Frank's new business had been in trouble for a while, and the signs were obvious that it was time to close up and do something else. Frank's father was a multi-millionaire, and because he could, he lent Frank a million dollars, but the business was never going to succeed, and receiving this money merely delayed the inevitable. Frank eventually found himself in even more debt, and with a bigger challenge on his hands.

It isn't necessarily a 'bad' thing when one of our pathways comes to an end. It can be the beginning of something new and exciting – if our attitude allows it to be so.

Their Low Point

Allow people to get to a point where they recognize the situation for what it is; it may be in this lifetime, or it may be the next. This may be hard to stomach, but many people need to reach a low point in their lives before being open to new ways of thinking – low enough so as to become motivated to try something new, to be open to a different viewpoint and advance in a new direction. It is by being allowed to go through their challenges that they reach new levels of *long-term* happiness. It is in our nature to help others feel better, but if people are constantly rescued from their situations, it delays their growth.

Allow Others to Make Their Journey

People can create challenges for themselves even when they are making deliberate changes in direction, because all changes have the potential to cause confusion and disharmony. As changes are made, the old must break down to make way for the new (see Chapter 24 *Letting Go of Your Past to Transition to Your New Life*). Sometimes, it can seem like they have made their situation worse, but if they bravely stick with the changes, the new life eventually arrives as planned. If you 'save' them, the changes are halted.

Achieving a Balance

During a period of change, people may initially swing to the opposite side. A victim can initially become a tyrant, someone who is tight-fisted may start spending extravagantly, and someone with low self-esteem may start bragging. Over time, however, they achieve equilibrium and end up somewhere in the middle. They must be allowed to move through all these changes in order to achieve balance.

Allow Others Their Freedom

You may try to compare other people's lives to your own, but it's better to realize that every person is unique, and they're each focusing on their particular areas that need growth. You cannot know the growth that is required by another person. Everyone reacts differently to every circumstance. People can learn from your experience, but their own experience ensures true understanding and wisdom. People become ready for their insights via the challenges they experience. Resist interfering if someone lives life differently to you. Grant others the freedom to be who they are and where they are today. They will move through these experiences faster, and then on to a new level of awareness. Acceptance is a great gift.

"Not until we are lost do we begin to understand ourselves."
Henry David Thoreau
(American author and philosopher, 1817–1862)

Help by Thinking Only the Best Thoughts for Others

The best way to help someone is by using the power of your thoughts to imagine their highest potential as they move through difficulty. When others are sick, you should endeavour to speak about them as though they are recovering quickly or already well again. Even though, in our society, sympathy means we care, displaying feelings of pity or hopelessness toward a sick person adversely affects their recovery. It is wise to keep certain issues to yourself so as to avoid other people gossiping or creating drama from the situation.

Perhaps it is Your Issue Too?

If another person's circumstance is adversely affecting you, have a look within to see if it is teaching you something. It is possible for people to create drama in their lives and have it as a reflection for you. Anything that has an emotionally unfavourable effect on you has your name on it.

Be an Example to Others

Consciously choosing a brilliant life for yourself is a wonderful example for those around you. Your high vibrations, and your inspiration, acceptance of others and support will nurture them and assist them in their growth. If someone is ready for learning, teach them the techniques you are learning so they can add their own power, freedom and happiness to their life.

Summary of

"Saving Others from Their Challenges"

- You may have the urge to help others if you think they are troubled, but love and support is all you should provide. If you save people from their challenges, you are delaying their growth and their long-term happiness.
- Everyone is in the ideal place for growth right now.
- Difficult circumstances provide people with motivation for change.
- Even when someone is making changes toward a greater life, they may experience some confusion and disharmony as old ways of thinking are replaced by new ways. There is a period of transition, which can be bewildering.
- Some changes cause people to become the opposite of what they were. It can be a shock to find a friend move from victim to tyrant. Over time though, they will work out a balance.
- It is best for each of us to have our own experiences and work through our own issues, as then we achieve wisdom and understanding about life.
- If someone's circumstance adversely affects you, be aware that it is a teaching for you.
- By living your life to the best of your ability, you set an example for those around you. You will inspire them to a greater life.

EXERCISE: How to Give Others

Freedom to Live Their Lives

1. As part of your support, allow people to ask your opinion. Try to be encouraging, hypothetical and general in your advice. Do not expect them to follow your advice. Your opinion may not be what they need right now, but it may plant a seed for action in their future when they are ready.
2. Support others by being objective. If they ask for advice, help them to see the potentials of their situation and provide ideas, but tell them they know what is best for them. Encourage them to go within by asking themselves what is best.
3. Remember, some people have not reached their low point, and perhaps are not ready to hear about taking responsibility for their lives.
4. Let them know you will always be there to love and support them. This helps them feel accepted. You can assist in a crisis, but avoid providing an opportunity for them to escape their issues. Once they start recognizing the issue for the feedback that it is, you can start adding a little more assistance. Always be mindful that you should stand back and allow situations to unfold.

CHAPTER 34

Changing Others by Changing Yourself

"Happiness is a choice that requires effort at all times."

Aeschylus
(Greek playwright, 525–456 BC)

It sounds easier for someone else to make changes so that you can be happy. That's less effort for you, right? You can see yourself sitting back with your feet up, watching the world dancing to your tune. Well, actually *yes,* but *you* need to decide the dance, and *you* need to decide the tune. If you want a new dance or tune, then again, *you* must change them.

Waiting for others to change means your power to create change in your life is held by other people, and they decide your life. No thanks. Fortunately, the only person you can change is yourself, because then *you,* and only *you,* hold the power to choose your life.

Most people wait or hope for others to change so they can get what they want, but this is a hopeless situation. Not only are they giving away their power, but what do they do while they are waiting? Stay miserable? I don't think so. In any case, forcing others to change is rarely successful. The change, even if it eventually happens, will be short-term and may not be optimal for you.

Back to *You*

Changing yourself is far more effective, because the change is tailor-made to your specifications, and there is no waiting involved. Other people *instantly* behave differently, due to your new thoughts, and their subsequent reflection back to you. If you think there is a quality missing from someone, the best way to achieve it is to create that quality in yourself. They will then reflect that quality back to you, *as if you had* changed them. Again, life is easier – you achieve your goal, you grow and you empower yourself. Just a little effort on your part reaps rich rewards.

Some people prefer absolute control of everything that happens in their lives. These people are often referred to as 'control-freaks'. There is usually a bit of that in most people. Parents often struggle with their children in this area when the parent wants everything done their way. A huge conflict results, until the parent has a light bulb moment as to what's really happening. Once the parent pulls back and stops using force, the situation usually evaporates.

I'm Only Happy When You are Happy

Sometimes, we want everyone around us to be happy before we can be happy. So, what...are we going to wait forever? It is a pointless mission. Despite whatever is going on around you, it is healthier and easier for you to *choose to be happy*. It's okay if someone is sad – they may be changing themselves to something greater. Changes can manifest as sadness if they are saying goodbye to a part of themselves. Even if it is someone close to you, and you need to help them, you can still be happy. And if you are happy, you're more of an asset to others; you'll naturally bring cheer to those around you. By changing yourself, you change your world.

"Change is the essence of life. Be willing to surrender what you are for what you could become."
Unknown

When You Don't Change You Hurt Yourself

Sometimes, those around you *are* trying to change, but *your behavior* interferes.

Anna was desperate for her husband, Peter, to change. Her major concern was that he'd started a new business, and as there was no income, she was forced to return to work when she would have rather stayed home to look after her young children. They were obviously having communication issues, but Peter promised her that the business would make them very wealthy. Anna wasn't so sure. One day, Peter received an offer to work in a friend's business for an extremely high salary. Anna could tell that her husband was tempted, and he asked her opinion. Anna secretly wanted Peter to take the offer, but her need to make a stand on her issue with the new business was too great. She told him that she'd leave the decision up to him, but she also told him to keep in mind that she would think he'd been lying about the potential of the new business if he took the offer. Of course, he felt cornered, and didn't take the offer...and Anna missed an opportunity to get what she wanted.

It's very easy to sabotage our dreams. Anna's dream was about to arrive, but her need to be proved correct got in the way.

You Be as Flexible as Possible

Strive to be as flexible as possible in your thoughts, beliefs and behaviors. By being the most flexible person, you always hold the power to get what you want and have the greatest freedom. You still focus on your goals, but you are sufficiently evolved to let go of controlling the outcome, and are therefore able to allow the most ideal circumstance to appear for all involved. The results you obtain will always be greater using this technique, which works in any setting, such as in families, in friendships, in sport and at work.

Be prepared to change yourself so that others are automatically who you want them to be. By doing this, you are using your power to evolve as well as staying on track to create any life you want.

Summary of

"Changing Others by Changing Yourself"

- ♦ If you wait for others to change so you can get what you want, you are handing them your power.

- Never wait for someone else to be happy so that you can be happy. What if they never choose to be happy?
- You can only change yourself and choose how you feel. You can't do it for someone else.
- By changing yourself, you hold the power to choose your life.
- As you change yourself, others automatically change. This is because you see your reflection in them.
- Focus on your goal, but choose to be the most flexible person in every situation. The more flexible you are, the more powerful you are. You get what you want and you enjoy more freedom.

EXERCISE: How to Get What You Want by Changing Yourself

Example:

If you want your partner to pay more attention to you:

1. List everything you wish your partner did for you, and how each one would make you feel if they did it. Use this to learn what you need to provide for yourself.
2. Move through the list and create an affirmation for each that says how you would like to feel. For example:
   - If you would like to feel more love and affection, say, 'I have all the love I want, and more' and 'I feel loved and noticed.'
   - If you would like to feel more appreciated, say, 'I put myself first' and 'I feel cherished, treasured and appreciated.'
   - If you want to feel more supported, say, 'I feel valued', 'I feel completely understood' and 'I approve of myself.'

This is very simple. What you are doing here is using your thoughts to activate another part of the brain where you already have what you want. This place in your brain already exists *now*, and starts to fire once you decide to access it. This method does not force your partner to provide more love and affection; it will simply happen because you are thinking it and creating it in you, and your partner is your reflection. Your thoughts create your experiences. Create as many different affirmations as you like – use your own words, and be sure they resonate with you and bring about a special feeling in you. Once they do, look at them every day and you will have the relationship you want.

3.   Ensure you are finding ways to be creative, and try new things. Take action by following up on your interests. Take responsibility for doing things that you find interesting, and that you enjoy. Doing something you love lifts your self-worth, and you will get all you want and more. People are drawn toward happy people. The more fulfilled you are, the more valued and loved you will feel.

It isn't our partner who provides us with care and nurture – we do it for ourselves, and then we get it from others as well. If our partner is forced to show us love, it will be short-term, and then we'll find ourselves needing to force another fix on them. Also, neediness and desperation usually push people away. It is immensely empowering and fulfilling to handle the controls in your life and to ensure that you give yourself what you want.

NOTE:
Our relationship with our partner is one of our biggest learning platforms. The more we love ourselves, the better our relationship will be. To achieve the results you want, you need to have your heart and soul in the relationship. If, after careful consideration, you realize you and your partner no longer resonate, then it is time to seek assistance such as counseling, in order to gain ideas and objectivity. Although our society frowns on breakups, we are all constantly growing and changing, usually at a different rate to our partner. To move on from your partner is perfectly acceptable if that is what you need to grow and be happy. It requires courage, and the transition is often painful, but if it is best for you, it is also best for your partner, even if they struggle to recognize that. If you find a new relationship, it will take you in new directions, to fresh knowledge, growth

and understanding about yourself and about life. This subject, of course could form the basis of another book, so I will leave it there. Just know that above all, your happiness must come first.

Example:

If you want your partner to give you more freedom in relation to time, money, hobbies, friendships, etc.:

1. Contemplate what freedom would provide for you. How would you know if you had freedom? What is freedom, and how does it feel?

2. Write some affirmations or create a story about already having freedom, and what you enjoy about it. This will only take 5 or 10 minutes, and you will unlock your understanding of freedom and what it really means. Just by writing a story, you already attract more freedom – because that is what you are thinking. Ideas will start to arrive to make this a reality, and your partner will appear to change as well.

3. Sometimes we think we need permission from others for our freedom, but other people cannot 'give' us freedom; we create it for ourselves. It is frequently our own limited thinking that prevents us from gaining our freedom, and all we need to do is find ways to get what we want.

4. As everything is in the mind, your attitude will ensure that you have all the freedom you need.

CHAPTER 35

Children

"Whoever teaches his son teaches not alone his son, but also his son's son and so on to the end of generation."

Hebrew Proverb

Children are also our mirrors. It is challenging to be objective with your children because of your closeness to them, and your thoughts also have a tremendous impact on your children. When speaking of your children to others, be vigilant about what you say. If you complain about your child's behavior, they will give you more of that behavior. If you discuss recurring ailments, they will continue to appear. What you focus on appears in your life – even in regard to your children.

Children Expect Mastery

Parenting can be one of the biggest challenges we face. Children expect us to be the masters of ourselves, but it is beyond question that they can be our greatest teachers. I wasn't aware that my patience needed work until I had children, but I quickly worked out that anger only escalates an already challenging situation. Children demand that you be the best you can be. Your children have your DNA, and so probably have some of the same issues as you. Children reflect to you exactly who you are, which is why we say they 'press your buttons'.

At the same time, children are a great way to check your growth. The more inner harmony I achieved, the more harmonious my relationship was with my children, and they, too, played more harmoniously together.

Communication Matters...Again

Communicating with children can be more challenging than dealing with adults. In a business situation, most employees do as they are asked. With children, extra effort is required to get our points across clearly in an effective, harmonious way. Children also have their own view of reality, and arrive in our lives without an understanding of respect and authority. They are relentless in getting what they want! We need to motivate them toward helpful behavior without forcing them into submission.

Anyone working with children is often instructing them, so it pays to choose words carefully, for example avoiding the word 'don't'. I've seen so many parents (and teachers) struggling to instruct their children and becoming immensely frustrated – all because they are using the word 'don't'. The brain works in positives, and if we say to a child, 'Don't touch the television', the child hears, '... *touch the television.*' It is the same if I say to you, 'Don't think of an ice-cream.' What do you immediately think of? Rather, tell the child what you *want* them to do. By stating it in the positive, such as, 'Stay away from the television', the child hears, '*Stay away.*'

Using 'don't' is such a deeply embedded habit that you may want to ask your partner or a friend to remind you if they hear you using this word. If you do use it and realize it, then follow up with a positively constructed sentence. This cancels out the negative. This change alone can radically improve your communication with children.

Children Also Create Their Reality And They Should Know This

"We need to teach the next generation of children from Day One that they are responsible for their lives. Mankind's greatest gift, also its greatest curse, is that we have free choice. We can make our choices built from love or from fear."
Elisabeth Kubler-Ross
(Swiss-American psychiatrist and author)

246

The information in this book is ideal for children. Continue to educate children as much as possible on this understanding of life. Show and teach them the advantages of respect, love and compassion. Tell them that other people are doing their best, and that the world they live in is a reflection of their own thoughts. Then let go of controlling their actions (except if they hurt other people or animals) and step back to a role of love and support. Some of the concepts in this book may be a challenge for children to grasp, but pretending that life operates differently or protecting them from this reality is not an option.

Children should learn about assertiveness and playing fairly, but they also need to know that other people are our teachers and, if they want to, they can benefit from the message. For example, when someone is nasty to your child, encourage your child to understand that other people are mirrors to their thoughts, and they get feedback from others because of their thoughts. Encourage them to accept the incident merely as information, and that it has nothing to do with the other person. Some children initially resist the information, preferring to adopt a victim stance, but over time they recognize the difference. This also means that if they say something nasty about someone, you can remind them that if they continue to focus on that, they will attract nastiness from others.

Saving Our Children from Their Challenges

Most bullying situations remain unresolved, but this knowledge provides a pathway. It is best to focus on the child being bullied, and to find ways to increase their self-love and confidence, rather than wait for the bully to change or to try to change the bully.

The child who attracts a bully is sending out that signal. The bully and the victim meet because they are drawn together. Both have issues – happy people usually get along harmoniously with others. Therefore, both the bully and the victim need assistance in working on their self-love, so as to attract happy people and interact harmoniously. At this stage of the book, this is surely a no-brainer. Know that this powerful knowledge can be used for anyone in any situation. Everyone's thoughts create their reality, even children.

If they are not ready to accept these ideas, let it go – if it is a mindset by which you live, they will eventually learn. As children get older and see the example set by you, let them handle the situation in their own way for maximum experience.

Parents usually want to iron out all the creases in life and save their children from experiencing any disappointment or hurt, but this is similar to saving people from their teachings and challenges; it only delays their growth. Teaching your children about creating their own life and taking responsibility for their thoughts means they can start *now* to be aware of the results of their thoughts.

Accept, love, support and care for your children, but avoid saving them. It can be heartbreaking for parents to watch children learn through bitter experience, but children must be allowed to exercise their choices and experience the results. By doing so, they develop priceless resilience and wisdom. It's better that they learn from these experiences while they have parental support.

Furthermore, be ready to catch any teachings that appear for *you* via your children. If another child bullies your child, parental or survival instincts often flare up. Your child's battles and disappointments can become yours. If so, it is your opportunity for growth.

Children Can Also Have Goals

If a child is struggling in an area, take action to deal with it by working with them to create goals. Encourage them to dream big, and reinforce the fact they can make magic happen if they choose. This can be in any area of their life, such as health, friendships, education, sport, and so on. When speaking about the child or with the child, choose language that indicates that the child is already achieving in that area, and choose to focus on what they are doing well. This is not avoiding the truth; these thoughts tap into the place on the quantum field where they are already achieving, and it also helps them pave the way to their chosen reality.

Celebrate Achievements

*"If you want your children to improve, let them overhear
the nice things you say about them to others."*

Dr Haim Ginott
(Teacher, child psychologist and psychotherapist, 1922–1973)

Use every opportunity to praise your children – this reinforces remarkable thinking and celebrates their ability to create their lives. When my children find themselves in any wonderful situation in their life, I remind them that they created it. The more my children get this message, the better they do in all areas of their lives. By understanding this, they are also more likely to embrace adversity as their own doing. One of my children recently recognized the 'mirror' situation when two of her friends had a disagreement. One of the girls had stormed off, and my daughter said, 'She was angry because she was being bossed around... but she does that to other people.' It was empowering for my daughter to recognize and interpret what was playing out in front of her. All our discussions suddenly rang true to her.

As always, mixed in with this is the need to be taught gratitude and to maintain humility.

Limit the Media

Another way to help children achieve their highest potential is to limit their exposure to distressing events, such as certain television programs. These events cause fear and insecurity. Rather, choose uplifting, light-hearted or educational programs. Especially avoid the news on television; much of it involves the tragedies of the day, which are hardly thoughts on which we should be focusing, or encouraging our children to contemplate.

Remember, the more you evolve, the easier parenting becomes, and as your children observe you achieving what you want, they, too, are inspired to create a fabulous life.

Summary of

"Children"

♦ Children mirror our expectations. It is vital to be vigilant about our thoughts when it comes to our children because of our closeness to them.

♦ Our children have our DNA, and therefore have many of the same issues as we do. Children demand that we be the best we can be.

♦ Use constructive or positive language when speaking to children. Say what you want them to do, and avoid the word 'don't'. If you realize you have used the word 'don't', then follow up with a positively constructed sentence.

♦ As with adults, avoid saving children from everyday experiences that will develop their understanding and wisdom. Teach children that they create their lives through their thoughts.

♦ Use every opportunity to praise children and instil empowering behavior.

♦ Teach children gratitude and humility.

♦ Help children to set goals and to word them in the present moment, as if they are already achieving them.

♦ Teach children that everyone is doing their best, other people are mirrors to their thoughts, and they can make their own lives happier if they are willing to learn about themselves through others.

♦ In bullying situations, both the bully and the victim need assistance to create happiness in their lives. Help them see the situation as a learning exercise for them.

♦ Avoid distressing events such as the news on television. Rather, choose uplifting, light-hearted or educational programs.

EXERCISE: How to Help Children

Reach Their Potential

Example:

If your child feels that they are having difficulty getting along with a teacher or another student:

1. Instead of listening to them complain every day, teach them to take responsibility by choosing to imagine a more ideal situation. Children are immensely powerful in creating their lives.

2. Create a story as described in Chapter 19 *Creating Your Dreams.*

3. As they fall asleep at night, they could imagine the ideal scenario with the teacher or student. Make sure they imagine this situation as happening now in their minds. It could be that the fellow student or teacher is smiling at them, or congratulating them on their work, or having a laugh with them.

Work with them to create a few affirmations and say them as they fall asleep, e.g.:

♦ My teacher is kind to me.
♦ The other children are kind to me every day.
♦ I am chosen for fun projects.
♦ I have fun at school with the other students.
♦ My teacher and I enjoy working together.
  The child will usually turn the situation around quickly.

4. In any situation, as for adults, encourage the child to take control and create the outcome they would like. Affirmations can be created for any needs of the child. Perhaps include some that deal with their self-love. The techniques in this book will also work for children. Because they are younger, and have fewer doubts and more innocent, clear belief, children can usually make their dreams become a reality very quickly.

Section 6

The Gift of Every New Day

"Discipline is the bridge between goals and accomplishment."

Jim Rohn

(American motivational speaker and author, b. 1930)

*E*very new day is a gift – a fresh opportunity for a wonderful experience.

Be Clear about What You Want Every Day

What you want should be foremost in your mind as you start your day. The dawn of a new day brings renewed inspiration and potential. Old habits, emotions and issues in society can lure you away from experiencing your dreams, so re-inspire and realign yourself each day. Your dreams should be exciting to you, and focusing on them each day will remind you of where you are going and keep you motivated.

Knowledge Is Power

You now have the knowledge and potential to master your body, fulfil all your dreams and hold on to the freedom that has always been yours. It is a golden opportunity you have in this life. At the very least, decide to make this life the best you have ever lived. Every day, your life *happens* – whether or not you are aware of it. When you are purposeful and focused, you can be certain your life will happen the way you choose. Life is a daily journey of learning to be aware.

Daily Activities

"Either you run the day or the day runs you."

Jim Rohn
(American motivational speaker and author, b. 1930)

Master Your Body Moment by Moment

Focusing on your dream every day reminds you that you are more than your body, your emotions and your beliefs. By doing this every day, you are gaining control of yourself and mastering your body. Centering your attention like this says to yourself that you are worthwhile, and you are instantly boosting your love for yourself. The more motivated you are, the easier it is, so find a way of doing things that you enjoy. A number of suggestions are listed below; perhaps you can try them all over several days.

Note that we often start out enthusiastically with new ideas, full of hope and possibility, and then the body gets bored with the routine, and tries to give up and regain control. Push through this, and you will feel the rewards for keeping your word and staying in control.

More Than You Do Now? That's Progress

Start small and build up. The act of choosing even a small exercise may require some effort, and then following through may also require a small effort. Although focusing on your dream every day is ideal, that might be too challenging at first, so choose something you can handle, such as focusing on it only every Monday and Thursday, and do this for perhaps three months – you can choose when to increase it.

What you choose can be as small as you like, but try to make it a little bit more than you do currently. Do whatever it takes to get you going. Never give up simply because you're not doing as much as you'd like. Even if you are a perfectionist, every step is progress. Too much too early means a shock to the body, which resists, and then you fizzle out, quickly becoming despondent.

Small exercises work initially, because the important objective is to consistently take action, and to learn to keep your promise to yourself. When you have developed consistency, and you are more disciplined, increase the activity. If you feel you have to drop it back again, do so, as this is always better

253

than giving up completely. Always, always, always be kind and encouraging to yourself, even when you were hoping you could achieve more.

Staying firm and focused is encouraging for you, and will help you to gently and steadily gain control of the body.

This can be done in numerous ways.

Choose one or two of the following activities that resonate with you:

Gratitude

The benefits of gratitude are instantaneous and amazing. You need only spend a few minutes each day expressing gratitude for the life you already have. You'll be surprised at how much you become aware of, when you decide to reflect on what you have. Perhaps you'll be shocked that you have overlooked so much in your life. Gratitude provides you with a panoramic view and attracts even more wonderful aspects into your life. When you are grateful for what you already have, it is easier to attract your dreams. Acceptance of self comes with gratitude because you are bringing to light the spectacular aspects of your life.

Gratitude tosses the victim mentality aside and demonstrates that you have no boundaries: you are free.

Review Chapter 16 on *Gratitude* for more inspiration.

Contemplation and Planning

Spend 10 to 15 minutes each morning bringing the day you want toward you. Vividly move through your day in your mind as if you are already experiencing it. By using your imagination in this way, you smoothly step through your day, planning each event, and because it has already become your life, you and your desired day resonate as one, and it unfolds that way or better.

This sounds like a great idea when we read it, but too often, when it's time to follow through, the body feels a little lazy and can't be bothered. The body can always find a reason to skip focusing when it just can't quite grasp the benefit. Remember who is in charge, and get creative in finding ways to motivate yourself.

You may do this lying in bed as you wake up, or if you enjoy writing, keep a journal while enjoying a cup of coffee or tea. You can choose to do this inside, or outside in the cool, peaceful morning air. Being outside helps you connect with the universe, and if it's early enough, gazing at the endless canopy of stars connects you to the wonder of who you really are.

Make it into something special that you enjoy. Ideally, you will turn it into a habit as important as brushing your teeth. Imagine going through your day behaving as the new person you have created. This person (you) has everything you dream of having. You are rehearsing your day, as well as reminding yourself of your goals. Imagine your day as wonderful, exciting and inspirational. As you move through the day, prepare it for greatness. You're inviting into your life all the people and situations that deliver to you everything you want. Keep this up, and you truly become this person.

Imagine that your ideal results are acted out in the meetings, relationships, health, finances, peace, love and happiness that you have today. Imagine new discoveries, insights, knowledge and marvellous people being part of your day. You get a head start on your day, and you get to relish all that is wonderful in it.

When you commence your day in reality, you will notice an obvious flow, and remarkable coincidences and opportunities popping up. Even if you do experience a challenge, you will soar through it with greater ease and awareness, saying to yourself, 'I become greater by learning from everything that happens in my day.' You are expecting to have a great day, because in your mind you've already had it. You're in the quantum field, and whatever you expect, you get. It's easy to have confidence in your day, because *you took responsibility* to arrange it. As you head out the front door, you step into your fabulous day. The quantum field takes your thoughts from the morning and reflects them back at you all day long. What a way to fire up your day – empowered and uplifted!

Focus

Focus on the symbols you created as part of your dreams and goals. They are instantly recognized by your brain, and fire the neurons you want. Study them just before you go to sleep, and again upon waking. You could include these as part of your planning session. Be present with them and acknowledge how special they are. These are your dreams.

Affirmations

Affirmations remind you of the new you, and keep you in this moment, in the *now*, instead of in the past. They keep you focused on your dream.

Affirmations have had a bumpy ride over the years, and have sometimes been criticized for not working. They do work, and are extremely powerful, but they won't work if you get impatient for results and stop your affirmations before any tangible changes have occurred. Further, people are so used to focusing on what they don't want that it can be an effort to change and think constantly about what they do want.

Every time you choose a powerful affirmation over a limited thought, you change your brain and make it more possible to think that way all the time. When you are completely in the moment, and focus on thoughts such as, 'I am happy and I have everything I want', those are the only neurons firing in the brain, and in that moment they are an *absolute truth* for the brain. This is exceptionally powerful, and is why we avoid using the words we are trying to move away from, such as 'sad', 'ill', 'bad', 'I can't', and so on. We want those neuronal networks to *fade away due to neglect*. Every thought counts.

This is a journey, and while changes have the potential to be immediate, there may be delays due to any doubts you might have, and due to lack of focus. You may be working on several parts of yourself at one time. Stay steadfast, be sure to maintain your motivation and keep your affirmations fresh and exciting to keep you interested. Never give up on your dream. Do whatever it takes to keep going.

Affirmations can be used in many ways. Create affirmations about any topic. Put them where you can see them, such as next to your workstation, in your bathroom, in the pantry, in the car.

Change them or re-word them occasionally so that they stay new and inspirational. They should uplift you every time you see them. Say them out loud and see each word separately in your mind. It also helps to write them out again each day. Engage all the senses. By *saying* them out loud, with feeling, you get to *hear* them and *see* them in your mind, while writing means you get to *see* them again, along with *physically feeling* the act of deliberately writing them. Saturate your life with your affirmations. The more you do, the faster your dreams appear. You can't say them too often!

Be sure that your affirmations are worded in the *present* tense, and not in the future. If you say, 'I will have the most enjoyable job', then you will be on track to get a great job, but it's unlikely to ever become 'now'. Instead, say, 'I have the most enjoyable job'. The quantum field is able to reflect to you that wonderful job you have *now*.

Ensure your affirmations are *realistic* enough to motivate you. There are two reasons for this. Firstly, you're more likely to stick with them if they seem possible to you. Once you have scored a few goals, raise the bar. Secondly, if the affirmations seem way beyond your reach, you might unintentionally sabotage them with doubt the moment you say them. Gently expand your body's ability to accept any possibility, and understand that baby steps often get you there faster. Your affirmations should be grand and stimulating enough to motivate change in your life without generating too much fear of change in the body.

Here are some more examples:

- I get what I want.
- Today is a brilliant day for me.
- I constantly attract inspiring people into my life.
- I have a passion for learning and evolving.
- I know what I want to do.
- I am inspired to create my dream.
- I get pleasure from putting my dream in writing.
- I enjoy planning my day.
- I find it easy to create my dream.
- I steadfastly focus on my dream every day.
- I am happy wherever I am.

- I love and accept myself.
- I accept people the way they are.
- I feel more powerful every day.
- I love myself more each day.
- I give myself all the love I need in every moment.
- I am powerful, strong and healthy.
- I am allowing and accepting to everyone I meet.
- I am grateful for my wonderful life.
- I am magnificently wealthy.
- I have the most wonderful relationships.
- I get along easily with everyone in my life.
- Every day I am safe and protected.
- I am fearless and I happily embrace my future.
- I am more aware of my thoughts in every moment.
- I am honest with myself and others.
- I am motivated to create new affirmations.
- I patiently stick with my affirmations and I experience fabulous results.
- My affirmations quickly bring about results that I recognize.

Increase Awareness and Wisdom

Select teachings from this book and include a different one each week for several weeks as part of your planning, focus, and so on, for example:

- Gratitude
- Acceptance and Judging
- Letting go
- Loving yourself
- Honesty
- Abundance
- Forgiveness
- Changing yourself

Choose something in your life that you are eager to change, so that you are motivated to start catching your thoughts and actions in the moment.

Create it as a goal by using the technique from Chapter 19 on *Creating Your Dreams*. Imagine how this change will help you in your life. You are training yourself into awareness. For every thought or action you catch, recognize it as an achievement. This is done one thought at a time, but every thought that is caught and expanded has a chain reaction through your life. This is developing wisdom. All progress counts. You may even find, as you tackle this goal, that you quickly determine other areas you'd rather handle first. Feel free to do so. This is why taking action is so important.

You only gain awareness and wisdom through taking action. Any mistakes you make will also add to your wisdom and move you closer to understanding yourself. Each step brings results, and each experience creates wisdom. Keep putting one foot in front of the other. Take it day by day.

An intention to remember your chosen teaching will increase your awareness of it. You can do this by placing affirmations and reminders around your house and workplace.

Keep a diary to maintain your motivation, and to remember when to move on to the next teaching.

Develop Flexibility in Your Mind

Reflect on your recent conversations or situations. Notice how they were handled, and whether there was anything you could have done differently. Avoid judging your thoughts or behavior – merely *objectively observe* them. In order to grow, you have to start with who you are today. Look at yourself honestly, and start with your current thoughts and behavior. If you want to improve them, love and accept yourself while you make changes. This exercise isn't so much about the specific thought or behavior; it's about being aware. Jot your thoughts down and then create affirmations to change that thinking. When you become more aware of your thoughts and actions, you gain the power to create your life deliberately. You can reflect while you're at home, or between tasks. Any small amount of time will do.

After moments of anger, jealousy, anxiety, self-pity, greed, and so on, notice your emotion as being one of survival. Anger manifests when your control is threatened; jealousy is caused by feelings of limitation, scarcity or lack of fairness; anxiety is a sense of having no choice; self-pity arises if you feel alone, unloved, powerless; greed is about scarcity –

never having enough, and wanting more prestige. You'll notice that they are linked, and are actually very similar. Further, they apply to most of humanity. Healing starts with being honest about yourself. The key is to learn about what triggers you into survival mode. Understanding yourself is significant progress, because when you grab an aspect of yourself and look it in the eye, you have already started the healing.

Morning or Night... You Choose

If mornings don't suit you, then you can do the above activities before you go to bed. Focus on your goals prior to sleeping. Imagine yourself already having achieved your goal as you go to sleep, such as already working in that dream job, being in a relationship with that special someone, easily completing that marathon, engaging your audience in that public speech, playing top tennis or golf, and so on. Remember to repeat your affirmations, express gratitude for the day and imagine what dreams you would like that night.

If a daily focus is too regimented for you, then choose something else to fire up your initial enthusiasm, e.g. getting up a little earlier to go for a walk, even if it is only a ten-minute walk. You may use this to get fitter, to contemplate, or both, but choose the days on which you will do it and stick to them. Find something small that interests you, something where you are motivated to have power over yourself, such as exercising or eating better. It is all related to being in charge of you. Each time your body does what you ask, you master yourself. Do whatever it takes.

Blessing Your Food and Water

Whether you're dining out or at a party with friends, the chances are you toast something with your drinks. The discoveries made by Masaru Emoto about the effects of our thoughts on water contribute to the long-lost understanding of the tradition of toasting.

In his book *The Hidden Messages in Water*, Masaru Emoto notes that the average human body is 70% water, and our livers filter 200 liters of water daily. Imagine the benefit to your body if you 'toasted' all your liquids and food. You can choose to allow everything you eat or drink to become any thought you choose.[4] Today you may select 'radiant health', tomorrow 'magnificent wealth', the next day 'love' or 'gratitude' or 'genius'...or you may choose to have all of them at once. You select what you say, and the water and food changes to match the thought. What a blessing!

Keep Learning

Read more books on these topics. Read something every day that expands your knowledge and inspires you about life. Continually learning in all areas of your life takes you to getting what you want.

Re-read parts of this book, including the activities at the end of each chapter. You always learn more the second time through books like this. This is because, as you break through to a new higher frequency in your life and learn more about yourself, you are more receptive to information you may have previously glossed over. Information you previously took on board takes on a deeper meaning, a subtle nuance. Once you have gained additional knowledge, you will also gain more from the exercises.

Section 7

Conclusion

It Is NOW up to YOU to

Create MAGIC

"You must live in the present, launch yourself on every wave, find your eternity in each moment."

Henry David Thoreau
(1817–1862)

You are filled with joy, you are free of your body's control, you know how to get what you want, and you are all you need for your happiness. You see your life as brimming with wonderful potentials. You enjoy radiant health, both physically and mentally. You are inspired, allowing, fair, honest and generous; you are objective in all situations, and you achieve the miraculous. This is who you truly are.

You've seen the pattern where every aspect of your life is about you and only you. Once you understand the pattern sufficiently, you can easily resolve any part of your life.

You Will Always Have All the Support You Need

You will always have all the support you need on your journey, and you also have the inner strength that you need in order to be true to yourself. Support is easy to acquire when your goal is to be the best you can be. You'll attract support from several directions, and you'll find it arriving in unexpected ways. We've spent too long blaming others for our lives and wanting others to live our lives for us. As you take the first step, you will be nurtured on your journey. It somehow feels as though the universe lovingly embraces you and rewards you for making such a noble choice. You are always loved.

You Are the Powerhouse of Your Life

To truly be empowered, you need to recognize that *you* are the answer to your life. *You* decide your attitude, and *you* decide the world in which you live.

Notice that there is a common thread in many of the activities. When there is an issue to work through, always start with yourself. Consider whether there is anything you can change. You'll find that you can resolve most issues without anyone else doing or changing anything.

Now Is Always Now...Do It *Now*

You now have an amazing amount of knowledge on this topic. The next step is to use it. Even if you decide to postpone taking action with this knowledge, be assured there will come a time when you are ready. Never be concerned with missing opportunities if you are not ready. When you are ready, every opportunity will be waiting for you...they are always there, and will always be there. That's the way the quantum field works.

As mentioned before, be mindful that deciding to postpone action is a choice you make, and until you *take action*, living your greatest life is on hold, and you won't get what you want. So, until then, be sure to resist the temptation to complain about any situation or consequences!

Your motivation to take action will increase when you start noticing daily situations that you wish were different and, of course, now have the knowledge to change them. You know that everything happens in this moment, right now.

"One day at a time – this is enough. Do not look back and grieve over the past for it is gone; and do not be troubled about the future, for it has not yet come. Live in the present, and make it so beautiful it will be worth remembering."

Unknown

If you have come this far, the changes have already begun. Now, take the momentum from this book and try something new today.

Now is always when you are most effective. Now is pure. Now is a blank canvas; so paint onto it whatever you desire, and you'll be painting happiness in your mind. You have endless opportunities because, fortunately for you, *every moment is now.*

The end of this book represents...

       ...the end of problems

       the end of disappointment

       the end of boredom

       the end of limited thinking

       the end of being stuck

       the end of conflict

       the end of frustration

       the end of blame

       the end of judgment

       the end of confusion

       the end of unhappiness

       the end of disease

       the end of worrying about how you look...

...and the start...

      ...of loving yourself
      the start of your dreams
      the start of happiness
      the start of new experiences
      the start of discovery
      the start of infinite potentials
      the start of optimism
      the start of being responsible
      the start of letting go
      the start of abundance
      the start of radiant health
      the start of awareness
      the start of dream jobs
      the start of taking action
      the start of conscious choice
      the start of freedom
      the start of gratitude
      the start of accepting others
      the start of the power of love
      the start of living NOW...

...the start of having anything you want...

𝒥ust   ℒike   𝒯hat!

Appendix A

Release Emotion Technique

Avoid labelling the emotion you are feeling, because examining it causes it to get stuck. We want the emotion to be free-flowing. Avoid feeling guilty or annoyed about it, too. Instead, celebrate the fact that you noticed it. Pretend you are a therapist helping someone with this emotion. They wouldn't get annoyed, would they? They would be loving, detached, matter-of-fact, and work gently at releasing it for you.

1. Pretend you are watching yourself with that emotion. Observe yourself as if you are watching a movie of yourself on a cell phone. You are now safely out of the action, and you probably already feel less of the emotion.

2. Now see the emotion as air bubbles of energy, starting to bubble around you as if you're in water, just in front of your stomach. Watch them bubbling up, up and up, till they get to the surface above your head. As they reach the surface, hear the bubbles 'pop' as they burst through the surface of the water, releasing all the energy into the atmosphere. If you prefer, you may also use your hands to gently encourage the imaginary bubbles to rise to the surface in front of you.

3. This is a simple, yet extraordinarily powerful process. All you need is the *intention* to release the emotion, and the job is done.

4. This process should take about 30 seconds, and you may choose to repeat the process a few times. The beauty of this is that you can pretty much do it anywhere. In the moment is best, because you want the true feeling of the emotion to be present in order to release it. Once you signify your intent to release it, the emotional reaction in that circumstance is gone forever. You have released the energy of that emotion from every cell of your body. You will feel instant relief.

5. If you are in the middle of an extreme challenge that lasts for days or months, repeat this process every time you have a harmful thought, or feel regretful, angry, depressed or confused. Remember to avoid labelling the emotion. Releasing the emotional energy is so much healthier than internalizing it or taking it out on someone, and you'll enjoy long-term benefits.

Appendix B

Suggested Reading

When reading any book, avoid locking onto conclusions. Consider the knowledge and try it but stay free and open, developing an attitude that there is always more to learn and that greater understanding continues to come. Choose new ideas that inspire you and grant you greater freedom; learning should be a joy, not an obligation.

I also recommend the books listed in the References and Bibliography sections.

Journey of Souls by Michael Newton, Ph.D.
Case studies of life between lives

Destiny of Souls by Michael Newton, Ph.D.
New case studies of life between lives

Memories of the Afterlife by Michael Newton, Ph.D.
Life between lives stories of personal transformation

Many Lives, Many Masters by Brian L. Weiss, M.D.
The true story of a prominent psychiatrist, his young patient, and the past-life therapy that changed both their lives

The Four Agreements by Don Miguel Ruiz
A practical guide to personal freedom, a Toltec wisdom book

The Genie in Your Genes by Dawson Church Ph.D.

Epigenic medicine and the new biology of intention (your genes don't control your health or happiness, your thoughts do)

Take Control of Your Health and Escape the Sickness Industry by Elaine Hollingsworth
An empowering health book everyone should read. It's sold 500,000 copies worldwide. It exposes the lies the food industry and drug manufacturing giants have been telling us for years and what you can do to lead an improved and healthier life.

DVD *One Answer to Cancer* by Elaine Hollingsworth
This DVD is packed full of amazing testimonials by people who have reclaimed their health. They have eliminated invasive breast cancers, deadly Ewing's Sarcoma, terminal thyroid cancer, bowel cancer and an array of skin cancers, even large melanomas.
Both items can be ordered via her website www.doctorsaredangerous.com

The Divided Mind by Dr. John E. Sarno
The Epidemic of Mindbody Disorders (To manage pain as well as stomach and bowel disorders, allergies, headaches etc)

Healing Back Pain by Dr. John E. Sarno
The Mind-Body Connection – without drugs, without surgery, without exercise

The Emotional Brain by Joseph LeDoux
The mysterious underpinnings of emotional life

Synaptic Self by Joseph LeDoux
How our brains become who we are

Molecules of Emotion by Candace Pert Ph.D.
The science behind mind-body medicine

Power vs. Force by David R. Hawkins, M.D., Ph.D.
The hidden determinants of human nature

Evolve Your Brain by Joe Dispenza, D.C.
The science of changing your mind

Suggested Reading

You Can Heal Your Life by Louise L. Hay

The Power of Now by Eckhart Tolle
A guide to spiritual enlightenment

Chicken Soup for the Soul (series) by Jack Canfield
101 stories to open the heart and rekindle the spirit

A Return to Love by Marianne Williamson

Don't Sweat the Small Stuff (series) by Richard Carlson
Simple ways to keep the little things from taking over your life

I am me, I am free by David Icke
A Robots' Guide to Freedom

Quantum Physics

The Self-Aware Universe by Amit Goswami Ph.D.
How consciousness creates the material world

Quantum Enigma by Bruce Rosenblum and Fred Kuttner
Physics encounters consciousness

Physics of the Impossible by Michio Kaku
A scientific exploration into the world of phasers, force fields, teleportation and time travel

References

[1] L. McTaggert, *The Field* London: HarperCollins, 2003

[2] *Ramtha: An Introduction*, Edited by Steven Lee Weinberg, Ph.D.: Eastsound: Sovereignty Inc. 1988

[3] Ramtha, *The White Book* Bilpin: The Great Work Publishing, 2004

[4] Ramtha, *A Beginner's Guide to Creating Reality* Bilpin: the Great Work Publishing, 2004

[5] B. T. Spalding, *Life and Teaching of the Masters of the Far East (Volumes 1-6)* Marina del Rey, Devorss & Company, 1986

[6] N. Doidge, M.D. *The Brain That Changes Itself* New York: Penguin Books, 2007

[7] S. Begley, *Train Your Mind, Change Your Brain* New York: Ballantine Books, 2008

[8] M. Emoto, *The Hidden Messages in Water* New York: Beyond Words 2005

[9] Ramtha, *From Chaos to New Realities* Yelm: JZK Publishing 1995 (CD set)

[10] J. Sams, *Dancing the Dream* New York: HarperCollins 1999

Bibliography

Dr H. Alder, *NLP – The New Art and Science of Getting What You Want* London: Piatkus Books 1994

S.Begley, *Train Your Mind, Change Your Brain* New York: Ballantine Books 2008

G.Braden, *The Divine Matrix* Sydney: Hay House 2007

E. de Bono, *Serious Creativity* New York: HarperCollins 1996

N. Doidge, M.D. *The Brain That Changes Itself* New York: Penguin Books 2007

M. Emoto, *The Hidden Messages in Water* New York USA: Beyond Words 2005

S. Gawain, *Creative Visualization* New York: Bantam Books 1985

B. Lipton, *The Biology of Belief* Santa Rosa: Mountain of Love/Elite Books 2005

L. McTaggert, *The Field* London: HarperCollins 2003

C. Myss, *Sacred Contracts* New York: Transworld 2001

S. Nichols, *Science You-nified* Rainier: ManyWorlds 2004

J. O'Connor and J. Seymour, *Introducing Neuro-Linguistic Programming* London: Mandala 1990

Ramtha

The White Book Bilpin: The Great Work Publishing 2004

A Beginner's Guide to Creating Reality Bilpin: The Great Work Publishing 2004

S. Roman

Personal Power Through Awareness Tiburon: HJ Kramer 1986

Living with Joy Tiburon: HJ Kramer 1986

Spiritual Growth Tiburon: HJ Kramer 1989

Soul Love Tiburon: HJ Kramer 1997

S. Roman and D. Packer, *Creating Money* Tiburon: HJ Kramer 1988

J. Sams, *Dancing the Dream* New York: HarperCollins 1999

B. T. Spalding, *Life and Teaching of the Masters of the Far East (Volumes 1–6)*
   Marina del Rey, Devorss & Company 1986

P. Twitchell
   Stranger by the River Minneaplois: Eckankar 1999
   The Tiger's Fang Minneapolis: Illuminated Way Publishing 1979
   The Far Country Minneapolis, Eckankar 1987
   The Flute of God Minneapolis: Eckankar 1999

D. Virtue, *Healing with Angels* Sydney: Hay House 1999

S. Wilde, *Infinite Self* Sydney: Hay House 1996

P. Yogananda, *Autobiography of a Yogi* Los Angeles: Self-Realization
   Fellowship 2006

Acknowledgments

My gratitude goes to all those authors of books I've read, who penned their empowering and inspirational knowledge so I could learn, apply it and gain fabulous realizations of my own. I have always marvelled at how the nature of books allows us to buy massive amounts of priceless knowledge for so little. Many of these books are listed in the Suggested Reading, References and Bibliography sections of this book.

My gratitude also goes to my mother, Joy, who is the best mother I could've had. She truly loves me unconditionally, is always encouraging and has always accepted my choices in life without judgment.

To my children, my two treasures. I had no comprehension of the meaning of unconditional love, until I met them. They have both done their jobs well in showing me who I am, motivating me to look honestly at myself, to change, to grow and become greater. And in doing so I've been able to love and accept them even more for who they are. Several points in this book come from my learning through them. I feel eternally blessed and grateful to have had the experience of my children in my life.

To my partner, for his patience and ability to love and laugh so easily, showing me by example what it is to be fearless, and that a light heart is the way to becoming greater.

Although most of this book was written prior to my learning about Ramtha's information on this topic, the knowledge I gained from him helped me tie up several loose ends and made the book wonderfully complete. I already knew life operated in this way because of my experience, but Ramtha's information (specifically regarding quantum physics) helped me understand why. And my appreciation too, for JZ Knight who is Ramtha's channel.

Heartfelt thanks to my friend Robin Waldie for generously proof reading this book with great enthusiasm and her ongoing love and support.

For the professionalism and integrity of Julie and her staff at Love of Books in Brisbane Australia, thank you for providing such an essential and unique service to authors.

Please visit my website www.janetpoole.com to ask questions about the information in this book, to learn even more about this subject or to tell me a story about an experience you had as a result of learning this information. Questions and stories are most welcome.

Index

Acknowledgments

A Complete List of Exercises from the Chapters in the Book